I0021997

C#.NET, ADO

AND IDE CODE

Dynamically driven code for IDE controls

Richard Thomas Edwards

CONTENTS

A small introduction

There are a lot of reasons why writing C#.Net code can be fun and lucrative at the same time. Customers want code to not only work, they want it to do more than the standard functionality suggests it is capable of.

This book is about taking both standard and legacy controls and making them work for you. In this series of books, we're going to be working with ADO, ADO and OLEDB, DAO, Odbc, OleDb and SQL Client.

This particular book uses ADO to dynamically drive the DataGridVeiw, Listview and shows how to use legacy controls such as the MSFlexgrid and the OWC Spreadsheet.

Also, because the IDE supports the use of the Web Browser Control, we are going to use the Listview, MSFlexGrid and Spreadsheet inside the WebBrowser control and populate it from inside the IDE.

With that said, my goal is to provide you with stable source code that you don't have to write over and over again. That way you can focus on taking the code provided here and then go beyond these standard capabilities these routines support and fine tune them for you and your customer's needs.

Basic connections and coding conventions
Getting the most from less work

Don't know about you, but I only want to write certain routines once and reuse them over and over again. So, when it comes to using ADO to make a connection, why not make sure the code is designed in such a way that all that is needed to make the code return a recordset is to pass over to the routine a connection string and SQL Query. That code would look like this:

```
using System;
using System.Collections.Generic;
using System.Linq;
using System.Text;
using ADODB;
using Scripting;
using System.Data;

namespace WindowsFormsApplication6
{
    class ClsConnect
    {

        public ADODB.Recordset
Return_Recordset_Using_Connection_Command_And_Recordset(string
cnstr, string strQuery)
        {
```

```
            ADODB.Connection cn = new ADODB.Connection();
            ADODB.Command cmd = new ADODB.Command();
            ADODB.Recordset rs = new ADODB.Recordset();

            cn.ConnectionString = cnstr;
            cn.Open();

            Object obj1 = new Object();

            cmd.ActiveConnection = cn;
            cmd.CommandType = CommandTypeEnum.adCmdText;
            cmd.CommandText = strQuery;
            cmd.Execute(out obj1, Type.Missing, -1);

            rs.CursorLocation = CursorLocationEnum.adUseClient;
            rs.LockType = LockTypeEnum.adLockOptimistic;
            rs.Open(cmd);

            return rs;

        }

        public ADODB.Recordset
Return_Recordset_Using_Connection_And_Recordset(string cnstr,
string strQuery)
        {

            ADODB.Connection cn = new ADODB.Connection();
            ADODB.Recordset rs = new ADODB.Recordset();

            cn.ConnectionString = cnstr;
            cn.Open();

            rs.ActiveConnection = cn;
            rs.CursorLocation = CursorLocationEnum.adUseClient;
            rs.LockType = LockTypeEnum.adLockOptimistic;
            rs.Open(strQuery);

            return rs;

        }
        public ADODB.Recordset
Return_Recordset_Using_Command_And_Recordset(string cnstr, string
strQuery)
        {
```

```
            ADODB.Command cmd = new ADODB.Command();
            ADODB.Recordset rs = new ADODB.Recordset();

            Object obj1 = new Object();

            cmd.let_ActiveConnection(cnstr);
            cmd.CommandType = CommandTypeEnum.adCmdText;
            cmd.CommandText = strQuery;
            cmd.Execute(out obj1, Type.Missing, -1);

            rs.CursorLocation = CursorLocationEnum.adUseClient;
            rs.LockType = LockTypeEnum.adLockOptimistic;
            rs.Open(cmd);

            return rs;

        }
        public ADODB.Recordset
Return_Recordset_Using_A_Recordset(string cnstr, string strQuery)
        {

            ADODB.Recordset rs = new ADODB.Recordset();

            rs.let_ActiveConnection(cnstr);
            rs.CursorLocation = CursorLocationEnum.adUseClient;
            rs.LockType = LockTypeEnum.adLockOptimistic;
            rs.Open(strQuery);

            return rs;

        }
        public System.Data.DataSet
Return_Dataset_Using_A_Recordset(ADODB.Recordset rs, String
Orientation)
        {
            DataSet ds = new DataSet();
            DataTable dt = new DataTable();
            ds.Tables.Add(dt);

            switch (Orientation)
            {
                case "Single Line Horizontal":
                    {
                        for (int x = 0; x < rs.Fields.Count; x++)
```

```csharp
                            {

ds.Tables[0].Columns.Add(rs.Fields[x].Name);
                            }
                            DataRow dr = ds.Tables[0].NewRow();
                            for (int x = 0; x < rs.Fields.Count; x++)
                            {
                                dr[x] = rs.Fields[x].Value;
                            }
                            ds.Tables[0].Rows.Add(dr);
                            ds.Tables[0].AcceptChanges();

                            break;
                        }

                    case "Multi Line Horizontal":
                        {
                            for (int x = 0; x < rs.Fields.Count; x++)
                            {

ds.Tables[0].Columns.Add(rs.Fields[x].Name);
                            }
                            for (int y = 0; y < rs.RecordCount; y++)
                            {
                                DataRow dr = ds.Tables[0].NewRow();
                                for (int x = 0; x < rs.Fields.Count;
x++)

                                {
                                    dr[x] = rs.Fields[x].Value;
                                }
                                ds.Tables[0].Rows.Add(dr);
                                rs.MoveNext();
                            }
                            ds.Tables[0].AcceptChanges();
                            break;
                        }

                    case "Single Line Vertical":
                        {
                            ds.Tables[0].Columns.Add("Property
Name");
                            ds.Tables[0].Columns.Add("Property
Value");

                            for (int x = 0; x < rs.Fields.Count; x++)
                            {
```

```csharp
                                DataRow dr = ds.Tables[0].NewRow();
                                dr[0] = rs.Fields[x].Name;
                                dr[1] = rs.Fields[x].Value;
                                ds.Tables[0].Rows.Add(dr);
                        }
                        ds.Tables[0].AcceptChanges();
                        break;
                }
            case "Multi Line Vertical":
                {
                    rs.MoveNext();
                    ds.Tables[0].Columns.Add("Property
Name");

                    for (int y = 0; y < rs.RecordCount; y++)
                    {
                        ds.Tables[0].Columns.Add("Row" + y);
                    }

                    for (int x = 0; x < rs.Fields.Count; x++)
                    {
                        DataRow dr = ds.Tables[0].NewRow();
                        dr[0] = rs.Fields[x].Name;
                        for (int y = 0; y < rs.RecordCount;
y++)

                        {
                            dr[x + 1] = rs.Fields[x].Value;
                            rs.MoveNext();
                        }
                        rs.MoveFirst();
                        ds.Tables[0].Rows.Add(dr);
                    }

                    ds.Tables[0].AcceptChanges();

                    break;
                }
        }

        return ds;

    }
    public System.Data.DataTable
Return_DataTable_Using_A_Recordset(ADODB.Recordset rs, String
Orientation)
```

```csharp
{
    DataTable dt = new DataTable();

    switch (Orientation)
    {
        case "Single Line Horizontal":
            {
                for (int x = 0; x < rs.Fields.Count; x++)
                {
                    dt.Columns.Add(rs.Fields[x].Name);
                }
                DataRow dr = dt.NewRow();
                for (int x = 0; x < rs.Fields.Count; x++)
                {
                    dr[x] = rs.Fields[x].Value;
                }
                dt.Rows.Add(dr);
                dt.AcceptChanges();

                break;
            }

        case "Multi Line Horizontal":
            {
                for (int x = 0; x < rs.Fields.Count; x++)
                {
                    dt.Columns.Add(rs.Fields[x].Name);
                }
                for (int y = 0; y < rs.RecordCount; y++)
                {
                    DataRow dr = dt.NewRow();
                    for (int x = 0; x < rs.Fields.Count; x++)

                    {
                        dr[x] = rs.Fields[x].Value;
                    }
                    dt.Rows.Add(dr);
                    rs.MoveNext();
                }
                dt.AcceptChanges();
                break;
            }

        case "Single Line Vertical":
```

```csharp
                {
                    dt.Columns.Add("Property Name");
                    dt.Columns.Add("Property Value");
                    for (int x = 0; x < rs.Fields.Count; x++)
                    {
                        DataRow dr = dt.NewRow();
                        dr[0] = rs.Fields[x].Name;
                        dr[1] = rs.Fields[x].Value;
                        dt.Rows.Add(dr);
                    }
                    dt.AcceptChanges();
                    break;
                }
            case "Multi Line Vertical":
                {
                    rs.MoveNext();
                    dt.Columns.Add("Property Name");

                    for (int y = 0; y < rs.RecordCount; y++)
                    {
                        dt.Columns.Add("Row" + y);
                    }

                    for (int x = 0; x < rs.Fields.Count; x++)
                    {
                        DataRow dr = dt.NewRow();
                        dr[0] = rs.Fields[x].Name;
                        for (int y = 0; y < rs.RecordCount;
y++)

                        {
                            dr[x + 1] = rs.Fields[x].Value;
                            rs.MoveNext();
                        }
                        rs.MoveFirst();
                        dt.Rows.Add(dr);
                    }

                    dt.AcceptChanges();

                    break;
                }

        }

        return dt;
```

```
        }
        public System.Data.DataView
Return_DataView_Using_A_Recordset(ADODB.Recordset rs, String
Orientation)
        {

            DataTable dt = new DataTable();

            switch (Orientation)
            {
                case "Single Line Horizontal":
                    {
                        for (int x = 0; x < rs.Fields.Count; x++)
                        {
                            dt.Columns.Add(rs.Fields[x].Name);
                        }
                        DataRow dr = dt.NewRow();
                        for (int x = 0; x < rs.Fields.Count; x++)
                        {
                            dr[x] = rs.Fields[x].Value;
                        }
                        dt.Rows.Add(dr);
                        dt.AcceptChanges();

                        break;
                    }

                case "Multi Line Horizontal":
                    {
                        for (int x = 0; x < rs.Fields.Count; x++)
                        {
                            dt.Columns.Add(rs.Fields[x].Name);
                        }
                        for (int y = 0; y < rs.RecordCount; y++)
                        {
                            DataRow dr = dt.NewRow();
                            for (int x = 0; x < rs.Fields.Count;
x++)

                            {
                                dr[x] = rs.Fields[x].Value;
                            }
                            dt.Rows.Add(dr);
                            rs.MoveNext();
                        }
```

```csharp
                    dt.AcceptChanges();
                    break;
            }

        case "Single Line Vertical":
            {
                dt.Columns.Add("Property Name");
                dt.Columns.Add("Property Value");
                for (int x = 0; x < rs.Fields.Count; x++)
                {
                    DataRow dr = dt.NewRow();
                    dr[0] = rs.Fields[x].Name;
                    dr[1] = rs.Fields[x].Value;
                    dt.Rows.Add(dr);
                }
                dt.AcceptChanges();
                break;
            }
        case "Multi Line Vertical":
            {
                rs.MoveNext();
                dt.Columns.Add("Property Name");

                for (int y = 0; y < rs.RecordCount; y++)
                {
                    dt.Columns.Add("Row" + y);
                }

                for (int x = 0; x < rs.Fields.Count; x++)
                {
                    DataRow dr = dt.NewRow();
                    dr[0] = rs.Fields[x].Name;
                    for (int y = 0; y < rs.RecordCount;
y++)

                    {
                        dr[x + 1] = rs.Fields[x].Value;
                        rs.MoveNext();
                    }
                    rs.MoveFirst();
                    dt.Rows.Add(dr);
                }

                dt.AcceptChanges();

                break;
```

```
                    }

                }

            return dt.DefaultView;

        }


    }
}
```

As you can see from this, the intention of this code is two-fold:

Create a connection to a database and return a recordset from the query that is also supplied to the function.

Time to start working with the various controls.

The DataGridview Control

I'm going to keep the discussion short and sweet. Below is the code for the DataGridView control:

```
using System.Collections.Generic;
using System.ComponentModel;
using System.Data;
using System.Drawing;
using System.Linq;
using System.Text;
using System.Windows.Forms;
using ADODB;

namespace WindowsFormsApplication6
{
    public partial class Form3 : Form
    {
        public Form3()
        {
            InitializeComponent();
        }

        private void button1_Click(object sender, EventArgs e)
        {
            dataGridView1.Rows.Clear();
            dataGridView1.Columns.Clear();

            ADODB.Recordset rs = new ADODB.Recordset();

rs.let_ActiveConnection("Provider=Microsoft.Jet.OleDb.4.0;Data
Source = C:\\NWind.mdb;");
            rs.LockType=LockTypeEnum.adLockOptimistic;
            rs.CursorLocation = CursorLocationEnum.adUseClient;
```

```
            rs.let_Source("Select * From Products");
            rs.Open();

            for (int x = 0; x < rs.Fields.Count; x++)
            {
                dataGridView1.Columns.Add(rs.Fields[x].Name,
rs.Fields[x].Name);
            }
            dataGridView1.Rows.Add();
            for (int x = 0; x < rs.Fields.Count; x++)
            {
                dataGridView1.Rows[0].Cells[x].Value =
rs.Fields[x].Value;
            }
        }

        private void button2_Click(object sender, EventArgs e)
        {
            dataGridView1.Rows.Clear();
            dataGridView1.Columns.Clear();
            int y = 0;

            ADODB.Recordset rs = new ADODB.Recordset();

rs.let_ActiveConnection("Provider=Microsoft.Jet.OleDb.4.0;Data
Source = C:\\NWind.mdb;");
            rs.LockType = LockTypeEnum.adLockOptimistic;
            rs.CursorLocation = CursorLocationEnum.adUseClient;
            rs.let_Source("Select * From Products");
            rs.Open();

            for (int x = 0; x < rs.Fields.Count; x++)
            {
                dataGridView1.Columns.Add(rs.Fields[x].Name,
rs.Fields[x].Name);
            }

            for (y = 0; y < rs.RecordCount; y++)
            {
                dataGridView1.Rows.Add();
                for (int x = 0; x < rs.Fields.Count; x++)
                {
                    dataGridView1.Rows[y].Cells[x].Value =
rs.Fields[x].Value;
                }
```

```csharp
                rs.MoveNext();
            }
        }

        private void button3_Click(object sender, EventArgs e)
        {
            dataGridView1.Rows.Clear();
            dataGridView1.Columns.Clear();

            ADODB.Recordset rs = new ADODB.Recordset();

rs.let_ActiveConnection("Provider=Microsoft.Jet.OleDb.4.0;Data
Source = C:\\NWind.mdb;");
            rs.LockType = LockTypeEnum.adLockOptimistic;
            rs.CursorLocation = CursorLocationEnum.adUseClient;
            rs.let_Source("Select * From Products");
            rs.Open();

            dataGridView1.Columns.Add("Property Name" , "Property
Name");
            dataGridView1.Columns.Add("Property Value", "Property
Value");
            int y = 0;
            for (int x = 0; x < rs.Fields.Count; x++)
            {
                dataGridView1.Rows.Add();
                dataGridView1.Rows[x].Cells[0].Value =
rs.Fields[x].Name;
                dataGridView1.Rows[x].Cells[1].Value =
rs.Fields[x].Value;
            }
        }

        private void button4_Click(object sender, EventArgs e)
        {
            dataGridView1.Rows.Clear();
            dataGridView1.Columns.Clear();
            int y = 0;

            ADODB.Recordset rs = new ADODB.Recordset();

rs.let_ActiveConnection("Provider=Microsoft.Jet.OleDb.4.0;Data
Source = C:\\NWind.mdb;");
            rs.LockType = LockTypeEnum.adLockOptimistic;
            rs.CursorLocation = CursorLocationEnum.adUseClient;
```

```
            rs.let_Source("Select * From Products");
            rs.Open();

            rs.MoveFirst();
            dataGridView1.Columns.Add("Property Name", "Property
Name");
            for (int x = 0; x < rs.RecordCount; x++)
            {
                dataGridView1.Columns.Add("Row" + x, "Row" + x);
            }
            for (int x = 0; x < rs.Fields.Count; x++)
            {
                dataGridView1.Rows.Add();
                dataGridView1.Rows[x].Cells[0].Value =
rs.Fields[x].Name;
                for (y = 0; y < rs.RecordCount; y++)
                {
                    dataGridView1.Rows[x].Cells[y +1].Value =
rs.Fields[x].Value;
                    rs.MoveNext();
                }
                rs.MoveFirst();
            }
        }
    }
}
```

The Single Line Horizonal View

ProductID	ProductName	SupplierID	CategoryID	QuantityPerUnit	UnitPrice
1	Chai	1	1	10 boxes x 20 bags	18

The Single Line Horizonal View

	ProductID	ProductName	SupplierID	CategoryID	QuantityPerUnit
▶	1	Chai	1	1	10 boxes x 20 bags
	2	Chang	1	1	24 - 12 oz bottles
	3	Aniseed Syrup	1	2	12 - 550 ml bottles
	4	Chef Anton's Caj...	2	2	48 - 6 oz jars
	5	Chef Anton's Gu...	2	2	36 boxes
	6	Grandma's Boyse...	3	2	12 - 8 oz jars
	7	Uncle Bob's Orga...	3	7	12 - 1 lb pkgs.
	8	Northwoods Cran...	3	2	12 - 12 oz jars
	9	Mishi Kobe Niku	4	6	18 - 500 g pkgs.
	10	Ikura	4	8	12 - 200 ml jars
	11	Queso Cabrales	5	4	1 kg pkg.
	12	Queso Mancheg...	5	4	10 - 500 g pkgs.
	13	Konbu	6	8	2 kg box
	14	Tofu	6	7	40 - 100 g pkgs.
	15	Genen Shouyu	6	2	24 - 250 ml bottles
	16	Pavlova	7	3	32 - 500 g boxes
	17	Alice Mutton	7	6	20 - 1 kg tins
	18	Camarvon Tigers	7	8	16 kg pkg.
	19	Teatime Chocolat...	8	3	10 boxes x 12 pie...
	20	Sir Rodney's Mar...	8	3	30 gift boxes
	21	Sir Rodney's Sco...	8	3	24 pkgs. x 4 pieces
	22	Gustaf's Knäcke...	9	5	24 - 500 g pkgs.
	23	Tunnbröd	9	5	12 - 250 g pkgs.
	24	Guaraná Fantásti...	10	1	12 - 355 ml cans

The Single Line Vertical View

Property Name	Property Value
ProductID	1
ProductName	Chai
SupplierID	1
CategoryID	1
QuantityPerUnit	10 boxes x 20 bags
UnitPrice	18
UnitsInStock	39
UnitsOnOrder	0
ReorderLevel	10
Discontinued	False

The Multi Line Vertical View

Property Name	Row0	Row1	Row2	Row3	Row4
ProductID	1	2	3	4	5
ProductName	Chai	Chang	Aniseed Syrup	Chef Anton's Caj...	Chef Anton
SupplierID	1	1	1	2	2
CategoryID	1	1	2	2	2
QuantityPerUnit	10 boxes x 20 bags	24 - 12 oz bottles	12 - 550 ml bottles	48 - 6 oz jars	36 boxes
UnitPrice	18	19	10	22	21.35
UnitsInStock	39	17	13	53	0
UnitsOnOrder	0	40	70	0	0
ReorderLevel	10	25	25	0	0
Discontinued	False	False	False	False	True

The Listview Control

Again, keeping the dialog short, here's the code for the Listview:

```
using System.Collections.Generic;
using System.ComponentModel;
using System.Data;
using System.Drawing;
using System.Linq;
using System.Text;
using System.Windows.Forms;
using ADODB;

namespace WindowsFormsApplication6
{
    public partial class Form4 : Form
    {
        public Form4()
        {
            InitializeComponent();
        }

        private void button1_Click(object sender, EventArgs e)
        {
            ListViewItem li = null;
            listView1.Items.Clear();
            listView1.Columns.Clear();

            ADODB.Recordset rs = new ADODB.Recordset();
```

```csharp
        rs.let_ActiveConnection("Provider=Microsoft.Jet.OleDb.4.0;Data
Source = C:\\NWind.mdb;");
            rs.LockType = LockTypeEnum.adLockOptimistic;
            rs.CursorLocation = CursorLocationEnum.adUseClient;
            rs.let_Source("Select * From Products");
            rs.Open();

            for (int x = 0; x < rs.Fields.Count; x++)
            {
                listView1.Columns.Add(rs.Fields[x].Name);
            }

            rs.MoveFirst();
            for (int y = 0; y < rs.RecordCount; y++)
            {
                for (int x = 0; x < rs.Fields.Count; x++)
                {
                    if (x == 0)
                    {
                        li =
listView1.Items.Add(rs.Fields[x].Value);
                    }
                    else
                    {
                        li.SubItems.Add(rs.Fields[x].Value);
                    }
                }
                rs.MoveNext();
            }


        }

        private void Form4_Load(object sender, EventArgs e)
        {

        }

        private void button3_Click(object sender, EventArgs e)
        {
            ListViewItem li = null;
            listView1.Items.Clear();
            listView1.Columns.Clear();
```

```
ADODB.Recordset rs = new ADODB.Recordset();

rs.let_ActiveConnection("Provider=Microsoft.Jet.OleDb.4.0;Data
Source = C:\\NWind.mdb;");
            rs.LockType = LockTypeEnum.adLockOptimistic;
            rs.CursorLocation = CursorLocationEnum.adUseClient;
            rs.let_Source("Select * From Products");
            rs.Open();


            listView1.Columns.Add("Property Name");
            listView1.Columns.Add("Property Value");

            for (int x = 0; x < rs.Fields.Count; x++)
            {
                li = listView1.Items.Add(rs.Fields[x].Name);
                li.SubItems.Add(rs.Fields[x].Value);
            }
        }

        private void button4_Click(object sender, EventArgs e)
        {
            ListViewItem li = null;
            listView1.Items.Clear();
            listView1.Columns.Clear();

            ADODB.Recordset rs = new ADODB.Recordset();

rs.let_ActiveConnection("Provider=Microsoft.Jet.OleDb.4.0;Data
Source = C:\\NWind.mdb;");
            rs.LockType = LockTypeEnum.adLockOptimistic;
            rs.CursorLocation = CursorLocationEnum.adUseClient;
            rs.let_Source("Select * From Products");
            rs.Open();

            rs.MoveFirst();

            listView1.Columns.Add("Property Name");

            for (int x = 0; x < rs.Fields.Count; x++)
            {
                listView1.Columns.Add("Row" + x);
            }
```

```
        for (int x = 0; x < rs.Fields.Count; x++)
        {
            li = listView1.Items.Add(rs.Fields[x].Name);
            for (int y = 0; y < rs.RecordCount; y++)
            {
                li.SubItems.Add(rs.Fields[x].Value);
                rs.MoveNext();
            }
            rs.MoveFirst();
        }
    }
  }
}
```

The MSFlexGrid

Like me, it may be old, but it still works!

```csharp
using System;
using System.Collections.Generic;
using System.ComponentModel;
using System.Data;
using System.Drawing;
using System.Linq;
using System.Text;
using System.Windows.Forms;
using ADODB;

namespace WindowsFormsApplication6
{
    public partial class Form5 : Form
    {
        public Form5()
        {
            InitializeComponent();
        }

        private void button1_Click(object sender, EventArgs e)
        {
            axMSFlexGrid1.Clear();

            ADODB.Recordset rs = new ADODB.Recordset();
```

```
rs.let_ActiveConnection("Provider=Microsoft.Jet.OleDb.4.0;Data
Source = C:\\NWind.mdb;");
            rs.LockType = LockTypeEnum.adLockOptimistic;
            rs.CursorLocation = CursorLocationEnum.adUseClient;
            rs.let_Source("Select * From Products");
            rs.Open();

            axMSFlexGrid1.Cols = rs.Fields.Count + 2;
            axMSFlexGrid1.Rows = 2;
            for (int x = 0; x < rs.Fields.Count; x++)
            {
                axMSFlexGrid1.set_TextMatrix(0, x + 1,
rs.Fields[x].Name);
                axMSFlexGrid1.set_TextMatrix(1, x + 1,
rs.Fields[x].Value.ToString());
            }
        }

        private void button4_Click(object sender, EventArgs e)
        {

            axMSFlexGrid1.Clear();

            ADODB.Recordset rs = new ADODB.Recordset();

rs.let_ActiveConnection("Provider=Microsoft.Jet.OleDb.4.0;Data
Source = C:\\NWind.mdb;");
            rs.LockType = LockTypeEnum.adLockOptimistic;
            rs.CursorLocation = CursorLocationEnum.adUseClient;
            rs.let_Source("Select * From Products");
            rs.Open();

            axMSFlexGrid1.Rows = rs.Fields.Count + 2;
            axMSFlexGrid1.Cols = rs.RecordCount + 2;

            for (int x = 0; x < rs.Fields.Count; x++)
            {
                axMSFlexGrid1.set_TextMatrix(x + 1, 0,
rs.Fields[x].Name);
            }
            for (int y = 0; y < rs.Fields.Count; y++)
            {
                for (int x = 0; x < rs.Fields.Count; x++)
                {
```

```csharp
                    axMSFlexGrid1.set_TextMatrix(x + 1, y + 1,
rs.Fields[x].Value.ToString());
                }
                rs.MoveNext();
            }

        }

        private void button2_Click(object sender, EventArgs e)
        {

            axMSFlexGrid1.Clear();

            ADODB.Recordset rs = new ADODB.Recordset();

rs.let_ActiveConnection("Provider=Microsoft.Jet.OleDb.4.0;Data
Source = C:\\NWind.mdb;");
            rs.LockType = LockTypeEnum.adLockOptimistic;
            rs.CursorLocation = CursorLocationEnum.adUseClient;
            rs.let_Source("Select * From Products");
            rs.Open();

            axMSFlexGrid1.Cols = rs.Fields.Count + 2;
            axMSFlexGrid1.Rows = rs.RecordCount + 2;

            for (int x = 0; x < rs.Fields.Count; x++)
            {
                axMSFlexGrid1.set_TextMatrix(0, x + 1,
rs.Fields[x].Name);
            }
            for (int y = 0; y < rs.Fields.Count; y++)
            {
                for (int x = 0; x < rs.Fields.Count; x++)
                {
                    axMSFlexGrid1.set_TextMatrix(y + 1, x + 1,
rs.Fields[x].Value.ToString());
                }
                rs.MoveNext();
            }

        }

        private void button3_Click(object sender, EventArgs e)
        {
```

```csharp
            axMSFlexGrid1.Clear();

            ADODB.Recordset rs = new ADODB.Recordset();

rs.let_ActiveConnection("Provider=Microsoft.Jet.OleDb.4.0;Data
Source = C:\\NWind.mdb;");
            rs.LockType = LockTypeEnum.adLockOptimistic;
            rs.CursorLocation = CursorLocationEnum.adUseClient;
            rs.let_Source("Select * From Products");
            rs.Open();

            axMSFlexGrid1.Rows = rs.Fields.Count + 2;
            axMSFlexGrid1.Cols = 2;
            for (int x = 0; x < rs.Fields.Count; x++)
            {
                axMSFlexGrid1.set_TextMatrix(x + 1, 0,
rs.Fields[x].Name);
                axMSFlexGrid1.set_TextMatrix(x + 1, 1,
rs.Fields[x].Value.ToString());
            }

        }

        private void Form5_Load(object sender, EventArgs e)
        {

        }
    }
}
```

Spreadsheet Control

Below is the code for that control:

```
using System;
using System.Collections.Generic;
using System.ComponentModel;
using System.Data;
using System.Drawing;
using System.Linq;
using System.Text;
using System.Windows.Forms;
using ADODB;


namespace WindowsFormsApplication6
{
    public partial class Form6 : Form
    {
        public Form6()
        {
            InitializeComponent();
        }

        private void button1_Click(object sender, EventArgs e)
        {

            axSpreadsheet1.ActiveSheet.Cells.Clear();
```

```csharp
            ADODB.Recordset rs = new ADODB.Recordset();

rs.let_ActiveConnection("Provider=Microsoft.Jet.OleDb.4.0;Data
Source = C:\\NWind.mdb;");
            rs.LockType = LockTypeEnum.adLockOptimistic;
            rs.CursorLocation = CursorLocationEnum.adUseClient;
            rs.let_Source("Select * From Products");
            rs.Open();

            for (int x = 0; x < rs.Fields.Count; x++)
            {
                axSpreadsheet1.ActiveSheet.Cells[1, x + 1] =
rs.Fields[x].Name;
                axSpreadsheet1.ActiveSheet.Cells[2, x + 1] =
rs.Fields[x].Value;
            }
            axSpreadsheet1.ActiveSheet.Columns.AutoFit();
        }

        private void button3_Click(object sender, EventArgs e)
        {
            axSpreadsheet1.ActiveSheet.Cells.Clear();


            ADODB.Recordset rs = new ADODB.Recordset();

rs.let_ActiveConnection("Provider=Microsoft.Jet.OleDb.4.0;Data
Source = C:\\NWind.mdb;");
            rs.LockType = LockTypeEnum.adLockOptimistic;
            rs.CursorLocation = CursorLocationEnum.adUseClient;
            rs.let_Source("Select * From Products");
            rs.Open();

            for (int x = 0; x < rs.Fields.Count; x++)
            {
                axSpreadsheet1.ActiveSheet.Cells[x + 1, 1] =
rs.Fields[x].Name;
                axSpreadsheet1.ActiveSheet.Cells[x + 1, 2] =
rs.Fields[x].Value;
            }
            axSpreadsheet1.ActiveSheet.Columns.AutoFit();
        }

        private void Form6_Load(object sender, EventArgs e)
        {
```

```csharp
        }

        private void button2_Click(object sender, EventArgs e)
        {
            axSpreadsheet1.ActiveSheet.Cells.Clear();

            ADODB.Recordset rs = new ADODB.Recordset();
rs.let_ActiveConnection("Provider=Microsoft.Jet.OleDb.4.0;Data
Source = C:\\NWind.mdb;");
            rs.LockType = LockTypeEnum.adLockOptimistic;
            rs.CursorLocation = CursorLocationEnum.adUseClient;
            rs.let_Source("Select * From Products");
            rs.Open();

            for (int x = 0; x < rs.Fields.Count; x++)
            {
                axSpreadsheet1.ActiveSheet.Cells[1, x + 1] =
rs.Fields[x].Name;

            }
            for (int y = 0; y < rs.RecordCount; y++)
            {
                for (int x = 0; x < rs.Fields.Count; x++)
                {
                    axSpreadsheet1.ActiveSheet.Cells[y + 2, x +
1] = rs.Fields[x].Value;
                }
                rs.MoveNext();
            }
            axSpreadsheet1.ActiveSheet.Columns.AutoFit();
        }

        private void button4_Click(object sender, EventArgs e)
        {
            axSpreadsheet1.ActiveSheet.Cells.Clear();

            ADODB.Recordset rs = new ADODB.Recordset();
rs.let_ActiveConnection("Provider=Microsoft.Jet.OleDb.4.0;Data
Source = C:\\NWind.mdb;");
```

```csharp
        rs.LockType = LockTypeEnum.adLockOptimistic;
        rs.CursorLocation = CursorLocationEnum.adUseClient;
        rs.let_Source("Select * From Products");
        rs.Open();

        for (int x = 0; x < rs.Fields.Count; x++)
        {
            axSpreadsheet1.ActiveSheet.Cells[x + 1, 1] =
rs.Fields[x].Name;

        }
        for (int y = 0; y < rs.RecordCount; y++)
        {
            for (int x = 0; x < rs.Fields.Count; x++)
            {
                axSpreadsheet1.ActiveSheet.Cells[x + 1, y +
2] = rs.Fields[x].Value;
            }
            rs.MoveNext();
        }
        axSpreadsheet1.ActiveSheet.Columns.AutoFit();
    }

    private void splitContainer1_Panel1_Paint(object sender,
PaintEventArgs e)
    {

    }
  }
}
```

Listview inside a web page

Yes, you can!

```csharp
using System;
using System.Collections.Generic;
using System.ComponentModel;
using System.Data;
using System.Drawing;
using System.Linq;
using System.Text;
using System.Windows.Forms;
using Scripting;
using ADODB;

namespace WindowsFormsApplication6
{
    public partial class Form1 : Form
    {
        public Form1()
        {
            InitializeComponent();
        }

        private void Form1_Load(object sender, EventArgs e)
        {

        }

        private void button1_Click(object sender, EventArgs e)
        {

        Scripting.FileSystemObject fso = new
Scripting.FileSystemObject();
```

```
        TextStream txtstream =
fso.OpenTextFile(Application.StartupPath + "\\Products.html",
IOMode.ForWriting, true, Tristate.TristateUseDefault);
        txtstream.WriteLine("<html>");
        txtstream.WriteLine("<head>");
        txtstream.WriteLine("<META http-equiv=\"Content-Type\"
content=\"text/html\">");
        txtstream.WriteLine("<META http-equiv=\"Content-Type\"
contect=\"text/html;charset=UTF-8\"/>");
        txtstream.WriteLine("<title>Products</title>");
        txtstream.WriteLine("</head>");
        txtstream.WriteLine("<body bgcolor='buttonface'>");
        txtstream.WriteLine("<object ID=\"rs\"
classid=\"CLSID:00000535-0000-0010-8000-00AA006D2EA4\" height=0
width=0></object>");
        txtstream.WriteLine("<OBJECT ID=\"ListView1\" WIDTH=1140
HEIGHT=920");
        txtstream.WriteLine(" CLASSID=\"CLSID:BDD1F04B-858B-11D1-
B16A-00C0F0283628\">");
        txtstream.WriteLine("      <PARAM NAME=\"_ExtentX\"
VALUE=\"14975\">");
        txtstream.WriteLine("      <PARAM NAME=\"_ExtentY\"
VALUE=\"7408\">");
        txtstream.WriteLine("      <PARAM NAME=\"View\"
VALUE=\"3\">");
        txtstream.WriteLine("      <PARAM NAME=\"LabelWrap\"
VALUE=\"-1\">");
        txtstream.WriteLine("      <PARAM NAME=\"HideSelection\"
VALUE=\"-1\">");
        txtstream.WriteLine("      <PARAM NAME=\"FullRowSelect\"
VALUE=\"-1\">");
        txtstream.WriteLine("      <PARAM NAME=\"GridLines\"
VALUE=\"-1\">");
        txtstream.WriteLine("      <PARAM NAME=\"HotTracking\"
VALUE=\"-1\">");
        txtstream.WriteLine("      <PARAM NAME=\"HoverSelection\"
VALUE=\"-1\">");
        txtstream.WriteLine("      <PARAM NAME=\"_Version\"
VALUE=\"393217\">");
        txtstream.WriteLine("      <PARAM NAME=\"ForeColor\"
VALUE=\"-2147483640\">");
        txtstream.WriteLine("      <PARAM NAME=\"BackColor\"
VALUE=\"-2147483643\">");
```

```
        txtstream.WriteLine("    <PARAM NAME=\"BorderStyle\"
VALUE=\"1\">");
        txtstream.WriteLine("    <PARAM NAME=\"Appearance\"
VALUE=\"1\">");
        txtstream.WriteLine("    <PARAM NAME=\"NumItems\"
VALUE=\"0\">");
        txtstream.WriteLine("</OBJECT>");
        txtstream.WriteLine("");
        txtstream.WriteLine("<script language=\"javascript\">");
        txtstream.WriteLine("");
        txtstream.WriteLine("rs.ActiveConnection =
\"Provider=Microsoft.Jet.OleDb.4.0;Data Source =
C:\\\\NWind.mdb;\";");
        txtstream.WriteLine("rs.LockType=3;");
        txtstream.WriteLine("rs.CursorLocation=3;");
        txtstream.WriteLine("rs.Source = \"Select * From
Products\";");
        txtstream.WriteLine("rs.Open();");
        txtstream.WriteLine("");
        txtstream.WriteLine("var n = rs.Fields.Count");
        txtstream.WriteLine("var l = new Array(n);");
        txtstream.WriteLine("for(var x=0;x <
rs.Fields.Count;x++)");
        txtstream.WriteLine("{");
        txtstream.WriteLine("    l[x] =
rs.Fields(x).Name.length;");
        txtstream.WriteLine("}");
        txtstream.WriteLine("rs.MoveFirst();");
        txtstream.WriteLine("while(rs.EOF == false)");
        txtstream.WriteLine("{");
        txtstream.WriteLine("    for(var x=0;x <
rs.Fields.Count;x++)");
        txtstream.WriteLine("    {");
        txtstream.WriteLine("        if(l[x] <
rs.Fields(x).Value.length)");
        txtstream.WriteLine("        {");
        txtstream.WriteLine("            l[x] =
rs.Fields(x).Value.length;");
        txtstream.WriteLine("        }");
        txtstream.WriteLine("    }");
        txtstream.WriteLine("    rs.MoveNext();");
        txtstream.WriteLine("}");
        txtstream.WriteLine("rs.MoveFirst();");
        txtstream.WriteLine("for(var x=0;x <
rs.Fields.Count;x++)");
```

```csharp
        txtstream.WriteLine("{");
        txtstream.WriteLine("    var ch =
ListView1.ColumnHeaders.Add();");
        txtstream.WriteLine("    ch.Text = rs.Fields(x).Name;");
        txtstream.WriteLine("    ch.Width = l[x] * 8.35;");
        txtstream.WriteLine("    ch.Alignment = 0;");
        txtstream.WriteLine("}");
        txtstream.WriteLine("var li;");
        txtstream.WriteLine("rs.MoveFirst();");
        txtstream.WriteLine("while(rs.EOF == false)");
        txtstream.WriteLine("{");
        txtstream.WriteLine("    for(var x=0;x <
rs.Fields.Count;x++)");
        txtstream.WriteLine("    {");
        txtstream.WriteLine("        if(x == 0)");
        txtstream.WriteLine("        {");
        txtstream.WriteLine("            li =
ListView1.ListItems.Add();");
        txtstream.WriteLine("            li.Text =
rs.Fields(x).Value;");
        txtstream.WriteLine("        }");
        txtstream.WriteLine("        else");
        txtstream.WriteLine("        {");
        txtstream.WriteLine("            li.SubItems(x) =
rs.Fields(x).Value;");
        txtstream.WriteLine("        }");
        txtstream.WriteLine("    }");
        txtstream.WriteLine("    rs.MoveNext();");
        txtstream.WriteLine("    break;");
        txtstream.WriteLine("}");
        txtstream.WriteLine("</script>");
        txtstream.WriteLine("</body>");
        txtstream.WriteLine("</html>");
        txtstream.Close();
        webBrowser1.Navigate(Application.StartupPath +
"\\Products.html");
        }

        private void webBrowser1_DocumentCompleted(object sender,
WebBrowserDocumentCompletedEventArgs e)
        {
            //ADODB.Recordset rs = new ADODB.Recordset();

//rs.let_ActiveConnection("Provider=Microsoft.Jet.OleDb.4.0;Data
```

```csharp
Source = C:\\Program Files (x86)\\Microsoft Visual
Studio\\VB98\\NWind.mdb;");
            //rs.CursorLocation = CursorLocationEnum.adUseClient;
            //rs.LockType = LockTypeEnum.adLockOptimistic;
            //rs.let_Source("Select * from Products");
            //rs.Open(Type.Missing, Type.Missing,
CursorTypeEnum.adOpenStatic, LockTypeEnum.adLockOptimistic, -1);


        }

        private void button2_Click(object sender, EventArgs e)
        {
            Scripting.FileSystemObject fso = new
Scripting.FileSystemObject();

            TextStream txtstream =
fso.OpenTextFile(Application.StartupPath + "\\Products.html",
IOMode.ForWriting, true, Tristate.TristateUseDefault);
            txtstream.WriteLine("<html>");
            txtstream.WriteLine("<head>");
            txtstream.WriteLine("<META http-equiv=\"Content-
Type\" content=\"text/html\">");
            txtstream.WriteLine("<META http-equiv=\"Content-
Type\" contect=\"text/html;charset=UTF-8\"/>");
            txtstream.WriteLine("<title>Products</title>");
            txtstream.WriteLine("</head>");
            txtstream.WriteLine("<body bgcolor='buttonface'>");
            txtstream.WriteLine("<object ID=\"rs\"
classid=\"CLSID:00000535-0000-0010-8000-00AA006D2EA4\" height=0
width=0></object>");
            txtstream.WriteLine("<OBJECT ID=\"ListView1\"
WIDTH=1140 HEIGHT=920");
            txtstream.WriteLine(" CLASSID=\"CLSID:BDD1F04B-858B-
11D1-B16A-00C0F0283628\">");
            txtstream.WriteLine("     <PARAM NAME=\"_ExtentX\"
VALUE=\"14975\">");
            txtstream.WriteLine("     <PARAM NAME=\"_ExtentY\"
VALUE=\"7408\">");
            txtstream.WriteLine("     <PARAM NAME=\"View\"
VALUE=\"3\">");
            txtstream.WriteLine("     <PARAM NAME=\"LabelWrap\"
VALUE=\"-1\">");
            txtstream.WriteLine("     <PARAM
NAME=\"HideSelection\" VALUE=\"-1\">");
```

```
            txtstream.WriteLine("    <PARAM
NAME=\"FullRowSelect\" VALUE=\"-1\">");
            txtstream.WriteLine("    <PARAM NAME=\"GridLines\"
VALUE=\"-1\">");
            txtstream.WriteLine("    <PARAM NAME=\"HotTracking\"
VALUE=\"-1\">");
            txtstream.WriteLine("    <PARAM
NAME=\"HoverSelection\" VALUE=\"-1\">");
            txtstream.WriteLine("    <PARAM NAME=\"_Version\"
VALUE=\"393217\">");
            txtstream.WriteLine("    <PARAM NAME=\"ForeColor\"
VALUE=\"-2147483640\">");
            txtstream.WriteLine("    <PARAM NAME=\"BackColor\"
VALUE=\"-2147483643\">");
            txtstream.WriteLine("    <PARAM NAME=\"BorderStyle\"
VALUE=\"1\">");
            txtstream.WriteLine("    <PARAM NAME=\"Appearance\"
VALUE=\"1\">");
            txtstream.WriteLine("    <PARAM NAME=\"NumItems\"
VALUE=\"0\">");
            txtstream.WriteLine("</OBJECT>");
            txtstream.WriteLine("");
            txtstream.WriteLine("<script
language=\"javascript\">");
            txtstream.WriteLine("");
            txtstream.WriteLine("rs.ActiveConnection =
\"Provider=Microsoft.Jet.OleDb.4.0;Data Source =
C:\\\\NWind.mdb;\";");
            txtstream.WriteLine("rs.LockType=3;");
            txtstream.WriteLine("rs.CursorLocation=3;");
            txtstream.WriteLine("rs.Source = \"Select * From
Products\";");
            txtstream.WriteLine("rs.Open();");
            txtstream.WriteLine("");
            txtstream.WriteLine("var n = rs.Fields.Count");
            txtstream.WriteLine("var l = new Array(n);");
            txtstream.WriteLine("for(var x=0;x <
rs.Fields.Count;x++)");
            txtstream.WriteLine("{");
            txtstream.WriteLine("    l[x] =
rs.Fields(x).Name.length;");
            txtstream.WriteLine("}");
            txtstream.WriteLine("rs.MoveFirst();");
            txtstream.WriteLine("while(rs.EOF == false)");
            txtstream.WriteLine("{");
```

```
            txtstream.WriteLine("    for(var x=0;x <
rs.Fields.Count;x++)");
            txtstream.WriteLine("    {");
            txtstream.WriteLine("        if(l[x] <
rs.Fields(x).Value.length)");
            txtstream.WriteLine("        {");
            txtstream.WriteLine("            l[x] =
rs.Fields(x).Value.length;");
            txtstream.WriteLine("        }");
            txtstream.WriteLine("    }");
            txtstream.WriteLine("    rs.MoveNext();");
            txtstream.WriteLine("}");
            txtstream.WriteLine("rs.MoveFirst();");
            txtstream.WriteLine("for(var x=0;x <
rs.Fields.Count;x++)");
            txtstream.WriteLine("{");
            txtstream.WriteLine("    var ch =
ListView1.ColumnHeaders.Add();");
            txtstream.WriteLine("    ch.Text =
rs.Fields(x).Name;");
            txtstream.WriteLine("    ch.Width = l[x] * 8.35;");
            txtstream.WriteLine("    ch.Alignment = 0;");
            txtstream.WriteLine("}");
            txtstream.WriteLine("var li;");
            txtstream.WriteLine("rs.MoveFirst();");
            txtstream.WriteLine("while(rs.EOF == false)");
            txtstream.WriteLine("{");
            txtstream.WriteLine("    for(var x=0;x <
rs.Fields.Count;x++)");
            txtstream.WriteLine("    {");
            txtstream.WriteLine("        if(x == 0)");
            txtstream.WriteLine("        {");
            txtstream.WriteLine("            li =
ListView1.ListItems.Add();");
            txtstream.WriteLine("            li.Text =
rs.Fields(x).Value;");
            txtstream.WriteLine("        }");
            txtstream.WriteLine("        else");
            txtstream.WriteLine("        {");
            txtstream.WriteLine("            li.SubItems(x) =
rs.Fields(x).Value;");
            txtstream.WriteLine("        }");
            txtstream.WriteLine("    }");
            txtstream.WriteLine("    rs.MoveNext();");
            txtstream.WriteLine("}");
```

```csharp
            txtstream.WriteLine("</script>");
            txtstream.WriteLine("</body>");
            txtstream.WriteLine("</html>");
            txtstream.Close();
            webBrowser1.Navigate(Application.StartupPath +
"\\Products.html");
        }

        private void button3_Click(object sender, EventArgs e)
        {
            Scripting.FileSystemObject fso = new
Scripting.FileSystemObject();

            TextStream txtstream =
fso.OpenTextFile(Application.StartupPath + "\\Products.html",
IOMode.ForWriting, true, Tristate.TristateUseDefault);
            txtstream.WriteLine("<html>");
            txtstream.WriteLine("<head>");
            txtstream.WriteLine("<META http-equiv=\"Content-
Type\" content=\"text/html\">");
            txtstream.WriteLine("<META http-equiv=\"Content-
Type\" contect=\"text/html;charset=UTF-8\"/>");
            txtstream.WriteLine("<title>Products</title>");
            txtstream.WriteLine("</head>");
            txtstream.WriteLine("<body bgcolor='buttonface'>");
            txtstream.WriteLine("<object ID=\"rs\"
classid=\"CLSID:00000535-0000-0010-8000-00AA006D2EA4\" height=0
width=0></object>");
            txtstream.WriteLine("<OBJECT ID=\"ListView1\"
WIDTH=1140 HEIGHT=920");
            txtstream.WriteLine(" CLASSID=\"CLSID:BDD1F04B-858B-
11D1-B16A-00C0F0283628\">");
            txtstream.WriteLine("    <PARAM NAME=\"_ExtentX\"
VALUE=\"14975\">");
            txtstream.WriteLine("    <PARAM NAME=\"_ExtentY\"
VALUE=\"7408\">");
            txtstream.WriteLine("    <PARAM NAME=\"View\"
VALUE=\"3\">");
            txtstream.WriteLine("    <PARAM NAME=\"LabelWrap\"
VALUE=\"-1\">");
            txtstream.WriteLine("    <PARAM
NAME=\"HideSelection\" VALUE=\"-1\">");
            txtstream.WriteLine("    <PARAM
NAME=\"FullRowSelect\" VALUE=\"-1\">");
```

```
txtstream.WriteLine("     <PARAM NAME=\"GridLines\"
VALUE=\"-1\">");
txtstream.WriteLine("     <PARAM NAME=\"HotTracking\"
VALUE=\"-1\">");
txtstream.WriteLine("     <PARAM
NAME=\"HoverSelection\" VALUE=\"-1\">");
txtstream.WriteLine("     <PARAM NAME=\"_Version\"
VALUE=\"393217\">");
txtstream.WriteLine("     <PARAM NAME=\"ForeColor\"
VALUE=\"-2147483640\">");
txtstream.WriteLine("     <PARAM NAME=\"BackColor\"
VALUE=\"-2147483643\">");
txtstream.WriteLine("     <PARAM NAME=\"BorderStyle\"
VALUE=\"1\">");
txtstream.WriteLine("     <PARAM NAME=\"Appearance\"
VALUE=\"1\">");
txtstream.WriteLine("     <PARAM NAME=\"NumItems\"
VALUE=\"0\">");
txtstream.WriteLine("</OBJECT>");
txtstream.WriteLine("");
txtstream.WriteLine("<script
language=\"javascript\">");
txtstream.WriteLine("");
txtstream.WriteLine("rs.ActiveConnection =
\"Provider=Microsoft.Jet.OleDb.4.0;Data Source =
C:\\\\NWind.mdb;\";");
txtstream.WriteLine("rs.LockType=3;");
txtstream.WriteLine("rs.CursorLocation=3;");
txtstream.WriteLine("rs.Source = \"Select * From
Products\";");
txtstream.WriteLine("rs.Open();");
txtstream.WriteLine("");
txtstream.WriteLine("var ch =
ListView1.ColumnHeaders.Add();");
txtstream.WriteLine("ch.Width = 120;");
txtstream.WriteLine("ch.Alignment = 0;");
txtstream.WriteLine("var ch =
ListView1.ColumnHeaders.Add();");
txtstream.WriteLine("ch.Width = 200;");
txtstream.WriteLine("ch.Alignment = 0;");
txtstream.WriteLine("var li;");
txtstream.WriteLine("for(var x=0;x <
rs.Fields.Count;x++)");
txtstream.WriteLine("{");
```

```csharp
            txtstream.WriteLine("   li =
ListView1.ListItems.Add();");
            txtstream.WriteLine("   li.Text =
rs.Fields(x).Name;");
            txtstream.WriteLine("   li.SubItems(1) =
rs.Fields(x).Value;");
            txtstream.WriteLine("}");
            txtstream.WriteLine("</script>");
            txtstream.WriteLine("</body>");
            txtstream.WriteLine("</html>");
            txtstream.Close();
            webBrowser1.Navigate(Application.StartupPath +
"\\Products.html");
        }

        private void button4_Click(object sender, EventArgs e)
        {
            Scripting.FileSystemObject fso = new
Scripting.FileSystemObject();

            TextStream txtstream =
fso.OpenTextFile(Application.StartupPath + "\\Products.html",
IOMode.ForWriting, true, Tristate.TristateUseDefault);
            txtstream.WriteLine("<html>");
            txtstream.WriteLine("<head>");
            txtstream.WriteLine("<META http-equiv=\"Content-
Type\" content=\"text/html\">");
            txtstream.WriteLine("<META http-equiv=\"Content-
Type\" contect=\"text/html;charset=UTF-8\"/>");
            txtstream.WriteLine("<title>Products</title>");
            txtstream.WriteLine("</head>");
            txtstream.WriteLine("<body bgcolor='buttonface'>");
            txtstream.WriteLine("<object ID=\"rs\"
classid=\"CLSID:00000535-0000-0010-8000-00AA006D2EA4\" height=0
width=0></object>");
            txtstream.WriteLine("<OBJECT ID=\"ListView1\"
WIDTH=1140 HEIGHT=920");
            txtstream.WriteLine(" CLASSID=\"CLSID:BDD1F04B-858B-
11D1-B16A-00C0F0283628\">");
            txtstream.WriteLine("    <PARAM NAME=\"_ExtentX\"
VALUE=\"14975\">");
            txtstream.WriteLine("    <PARAM NAME=\"_ExtentY\"
VALUE=\"7408\">");
            txtstream.WriteLine("    <PARAM NAME=\"View\"
VALUE=\"3\">");
```

```
            txtstream.WriteLine("    <PARAM NAME=\"LabelWrap\"
VALUE=\"-1\">");
            txtstream.WriteLine("    <PARAM
NAME=\"HideSelection\" VALUE=\"-1\">");
            txtstream.WriteLine("    <PARAM
NAME=\"FullRowSelect\" VALUE=\"-1\">");
            txtstream.WriteLine("    <PARAM NAME=\"GridLines\"
VALUE=\"-1\">");
            txtstream.WriteLine("    <PARAM NAME=\"HotTracking\"
VALUE=\"-1\">");
            txtstream.WriteLine("    <PARAM
NAME=\"HoverSelection\" VALUE=\"-1\">");
            txtstream.WriteLine("    <PARAM NAME=\"_Version\"
VALUE=\"393217\">");
            txtstream.WriteLine("    <PARAM NAME=\"ForeColor\"
VALUE=\"-2147483640\">");
            txtstream.WriteLine("    <PARAM NAME=\"BackColor\"
VALUE=\"-2147483643\">");
            txtstream.WriteLine("    <PARAM NAME=\"BorderStyle\"
VALUE=\"1\">");
            txtstream.WriteLine("    <PARAM NAME=\"Appearance\"
VALUE=\"1\">");
            txtstream.WriteLine("    <PARAM NAME=\"NumItems\"
VALUE=\"0\">");
            txtstream.WriteLine("</OBJECT>");
            txtstream.WriteLine("");
            txtstream.WriteLine("<script
language=\"javascript\">");
            txtstream.WriteLine("");
            txtstream.WriteLine("rs.ActiveConnection =
\"Provider=Microsoft.Jet.OleDb.4.0;Data Source =
C:\\\\NWind.mdb;\";");
            txtstream.WriteLine("rs.LockType=3;");
            txtstream.WriteLine("rs.CursorLocation=3;");
            txtstream.WriteLine("rs.Source = \"Select * From
Products\";");
            txtstream.WriteLine("rs.Open();");
            txtstream.WriteLine("");
            txtstream.WriteLine("var names = 0;");
            txtstream.WriteLine("var n = rs.RecordCount;");
            txtstream.WriteLine("var values = new Array(n);");
            txtstream.WriteLine("for(var y=0;y <
rs.RecordCount;y++)");
            txtstream.WriteLine("{");
            txtstream.WriteLine("    values[y] = 0;");
```

```
            txtstream.WriteLine("}");
            txtstream.WriteLine("");
            txtstream.WriteLine("for(var x=0;x <
rs.Fields.Count;x++)");
            txtstream.WriteLine("{");
            txtstream.WriteLine("    if(names <
rs.Fields(x).Name.length)");
            txtstream.WriteLine("    {");
            txtstream.WriteLine("        names =
rs.Fields(x).Name.length;");
            txtstream.WriteLine("    }");
            txtstream.WriteLine("}");
            txtstream.WriteLine("var ch =
ListView1.ColumnHeaders.Add();");
            txtstream.WriteLine("ch.Text = \"\";");
            txtstream.WriteLine("ch.Width = names * 8.35;");
            txtstream.WriteLine("ch.Alignment = 0;");
            txtstream.WriteLine("");
            txtstream.WriteLine("rs.MoveFirst();");
            txtstream.WriteLine("for(var y=0;y <
rs.RecordCount;y++)");
            txtstream.WriteLine("{");
            txtstream.WriteLine("    for(var x=0;x <
rs.Fields.Count;x++)");
            txtstream.WriteLine("    {");
            txtstream.WriteLine("        if(values[y] <
rs.Fields(x).Name.length)");
            txtstream.WriteLine("        {");
            txtstream.WriteLine("            values[y] =
rs.Fields(x).Name.length;");
            txtstream.WriteLine("        }");
            txtstream.WriteLine("    }");
            txtstream.WriteLine("    rs.MoveNext();");
            txtstream.WriteLine("}");


            txtstream.WriteLine("for(var y=0;y <
rs.RecordCount;y++)");
            txtstream.WriteLine("{");
            txtstream.WriteLine("    var ch =
ListView1.ColumnHeaders.Add();");
            txtstream.WriteLine("    ch.Text = \"\";");
            txtstream.WriteLine("    ch.Width = values[y] *
8.35;");
            txtstream.WriteLine("    ch.Alignment = 0;");
```

```
        txtstream.WriteLine("}");


        txtstream.WriteLine("var li;");
        txtstream.WriteLine("var z = 1;");
        txtstream.WriteLine("for(var x=0;x <
rs.Fields.Count;x++)");
        txtstream.WriteLine("{");
        txtstream.WriteLine("    li =
ListView1.ListItems.Add();");
        txtstream.WriteLine("    li.Text =
rs.Fields(x).Name;");
        txtstream.WriteLine("    rs.MoveFirst();");
        txtstream.WriteLine("    while(rs.EOF == false)");
        txtstream.WriteLine("    {");
        txtstream.WriteLine("        li.SubItems(z) =
rs.Fields(x).Value;");
        txtstream.WriteLine("        z=z+1;");
        txtstream.WriteLine("        rs.MoveNext();");
        txtstream.WriteLine("    }");
        txtstream.WriteLine("    z=1;");
        txtstream.WriteLine("}");
        txtstream.WriteLine("</script>");
        txtstream.WriteLine("</body>");
        txtstream.WriteLine("</html>");
        txtstream.Close();
        webBrowser1.Navigate(Application.StartupPath +
"\\Products.html");
    }
  }
}
```

MSFlexgrid inside a Web Page

Below is the code to do it:

```csharp
using System;
using System.Collections.Generic;
using System.ComponentModel;
using System.Data;
using System.Drawing;
using System.Linq;
using System.Text;
using System.Windows.Forms;
using Scripting;

namespace WindowsFormsApplication6
{
    public partial class Form7 : Form
    {
        public Form7()
        {
            InitializeComponent();
        }

        private void button1_Click(object sender, EventArgs e)
        {
        FileSystemObject fso = new FileSystemObject();
        TextStream  txtstream =
fso.OpenTextFile(Application.StartupPath + "\\Products.html",
IOMode.ForWriting, true, Tristate.TristateUseDefault);
        txtstream.WriteLine("<html>");
```

```
        txtstream.WriteLine("<head>");
        txtstream.WriteLine("<META http-equiv=\"Content-Type\"
content=\"text/html\">");
        txtstream.WriteLine("<META http-equiv=\"Content-Type\"
contect=\"text/html;charset=UTF-8\"/>");
        txtstream.WriteLine("<title>Products</title>");
        txtstream.WriteLine("</head>");
        txtstream.WriteLine("<body bgcolor='buttonface'>");
        txtstream.WriteLine("<object ID=\"rs\"
classid=\"CLSID:00000535-0000-0010-8000-00AA006D2EA4\" height=0
width=0></object>");
        txtstream.WriteLine("<object ID=\"MSFlexgrid1\"
CLASSID=\"CLSID:6262D3A0-531B-11CF-91F6-C2863C385E30\" height=915
width=1140></OBJECT>");
        txtstream.WriteLine("<script language=\"javascript\">");
        txtstream.WriteLine("");
        txtstream.WriteLine("rs.ActiveConnection =
\"Provider=Microsoft.Jet.OleDb.4.0;Data Source =
C:\\\\NWind.mdb;\";");
        txtstream.WriteLine("rs.LockType=3;");
        txtstream.WriteLine("rs.CursorLocation=3;");
        txtstream.WriteLine("rs.Source = \"Select * From
Products\";");
        txtstream.WriteLine("rs.Open();");
        txtstream.WriteLine("");
        txtstream.WriteLine("MSFlexgrid1.cols = rs.Fields.Count +
1;");
        txtstream.WriteLine("MSFlexgrid1.Rows = 1;");
        txtstream.WriteLine("");
        txtstream.WriteLine("for (var x = 0; x < rs.Fields.Count;
x++)");
        txtstream.WriteLine("{");
        txtstream.WriteLine("    MSFlexgrid1.Row = 0;");
        txtstream.WriteLine("    MSFlexgrid1.Col = x + 1;");
        txtstream.WriteLine("    MSFlexgrid1.Text =
rs.Fields(x).Name;");
        txtstream.WriteLine("    MSFlexgrid1.Row = 1;");
        txtstream.WriteLine("    MSFlexgrid1.Col = x + 1;");
        txtstream.WriteLine("    MSFlexgrid1.Text =
rs.Fields(x).Value;");
        txtstream.WriteLine("}");
        txtstream.WriteLine("</script>");
        txtstream.WriteLine("</body>");
        txtstream.WriteLine("</html>");
        txtstream.Close();
```

```csharp
        webBrowser1.Navigate(Application.StartupPath +
"\\Products.html");
        }

        private void button3_Click(object sender, EventArgs e)
        {
            FileSystemObject fso = new FileSystemObject();
            TextStream txtstream =
fso.OpenTextFile(Application.StartupPath + "\\Products.html",
IOMode.ForWriting, true, Tristate.TristateUseDefault);
            txtstream.WriteLine("<html>");
            txtstream.WriteLine("<head>");
            txtstream.WriteLine("<META http-equiv=\"Content-
Type\" content=\"text/html\">");
            txtstream.WriteLine("<META http-equiv=\"Content-
Type\" contect=\"text/html;charset=UTF-8\"/>");
            txtstream.WriteLine("<title>Products</title>");
            txtstream.WriteLine("</head>");
            txtstream.WriteLine("<body bgcolor='buttonface'>");
            txtstream.WriteLine("<object ID=\"rs\"
classid=\"CLSID:00000535-0000-0010-8000-00AA006D2EA4\" height=0
width=0></object>");
            txtstream.WriteLine("<object ID=\"MSFlexgrid1\"
CLASSID=\"CLSID:6262D3A0-531B-11CF-91F6-C2863C385E30\" height=915
width=1140></OBJECT>");
            txtstream.WriteLine("<script
language=\"javascript\">");
            txtstream.WriteLine("");
            txtstream.WriteLine("rs.ActiveConnection =
\"Provider=Microsoft.Jet.OleDb.4.0;Data Source =
C:\\\\NWind.mdb;\";");
            txtstream.WriteLine("rs.LockType=3;");
            txtstream.WriteLine("rs.CursorLocation=3;");
            txtstream.WriteLine("rs.Source = \"Select * From
Products\";");
            txtstream.WriteLine("rs.Open();");
            txtstream.WriteLine("");
            txtstream.WriteLine("MSFlexgrid1.cols = 1;");
            txtstream.WriteLine("MSFlexgrid1.Rows =
rs.Fields.Count + 1;");
            txtstream.WriteLine("");
            txtstream.WriteLine("for (var x = 0; x <
rs.Fields.Count; x++)");
            txtstream.WriteLine("{");
            txtstream.WriteLine("    MSFlexgrid1.Col = 0;");
```

```csharp
            txtstream.WriteLine("     MSFlexgrid1.Row = x + 1;");
            txtstream.WriteLine("     MSFlexgrid1.Text =
rs.Fields(x).Name;");
            txtstream.WriteLine("     MSFlexgrid1.Col = 1;");
            txtstream.WriteLine("     MSFlexgrid1.Row = x + 1;");
            txtstream.WriteLine("     MSFlexgrid1.Text =
rs.Fields(x).Value;");
            txtstream.WriteLine("}");
            txtstream.WriteLine("</script>");
            txtstream.WriteLine("</body>");
            txtstream.WriteLine("</html>");
            txtstream.Close();
            webBrowser1.Navigate(Application.StartupPath +
"\\Products.html");
        }

        private void button2_Click(object sender, EventArgs e)
        {
            FileSystemObject fso = new FileSystemObject();
            TextStream txtstream =
fso.OpenTextFile(Application.StartupPath + "\\Products.html",
IOMode.ForWriting, true, Tristate.TristateUseDefault);
            txtstream.WriteLine("<html>");
            txtstream.WriteLine("<head>");
            txtstream.WriteLine("<META http-equiv=\"Content-
Type\" content=\"text/html\">");
            txtstream.WriteLine("<META http-equiv=\"Content-
Type\" contect=\"text/html;charset=UTF-8\"/>");
            txtstream.WriteLine("<title>Products</title>");
            txtstream.WriteLine("</head>");
            txtstream.WriteLine("<body bgcolor='buttonface'>");
            txtstream.WriteLine("<object ID=\"rs\"
classid=\"CLSID:00000535-0000-0010-8000-00AA006D2EA4\" height=0
width=0></object>");
            txtstream.WriteLine("<object ID=\"MSFlexgrid1\"
CLASSID=\"CLSID:6262D3A0-531B-11CF-91F6-C2863C385E30\" height=915
width=1140></OBJECT>");
            txtstream.WriteLine("<script
language=\"javascript\">");
            txtstream.WriteLine("");
            txtstream.WriteLine("rs.ActiveConnection =
\"Provider=Microsoft.Jet.OleDb.4.0;Data Source =
C:\\\\NWind.mdb;\";");
            txtstream.WriteLine("rs.LockType=3;");
            txtstream.WriteLine("rs.CursorLocation=3;");
```

```csharp
            txtstream.WriteLine("rs.Source = \"Select * From
Products\";");
            txtstream.WriteLine("rs.Open();");
            txtstream.WriteLine("");
            txtstream.WriteLine("MSFlexgrid1.cols =
rs.Fields.Count + 1;");
            txtstream.WriteLine("MSFlexgrid1.Rows =
rs.RecordCount + 1;");
            txtstream.WriteLine("");
            txtstream.WriteLine("for (var x = 0; x <
rs.Fields.Count; x++)");
            txtstream.WriteLine("{");
            txtstream.WriteLine("    MSFlexgrid1.Row = 0;");
            txtstream.WriteLine("    MSFlexgrid1.Col = x + 1;");
            txtstream.WriteLine("    MSFlexgrid1.Text =
rs.Fields(x).Name;");
            txtstream.WriteLine("}");
            txtstream.WriteLine("for (var y = 0; y <
rs.RecordCount; y++)");
            txtstream.WriteLine("{");
            txtstream.WriteLine("    for (var x = 0; x <
rs.Fields.Count; x++)");
            txtstream.WriteLine("    {");
            txtstream.WriteLine("        MSFlexgrid1.Row = y +
1;");
            txtstream.WriteLine("        MSFlexgrid1.Col = x +
1;");
            txtstream.WriteLine("        MSFlexgrid1.Text =
rs.Fields(x).Value;");
            txtstream.WriteLine("    }");
            txtstream.WriteLine("    rs.MoveNext();");
            txtstream.WriteLine("}");
            txtstream.WriteLine("</script>");
            txtstream.WriteLine("</body>");
            txtstream.WriteLine("</html>");
            txtstream.Close();
            webBrowser1.Navigate(Application.StartupPath +
"\\Products.html");
        }

        private void button4_Click(object sender, EventArgs e)
        {
            FileSystemObject fso = new FileSystemObject();
```

```
            TextStream txtstream =
fso.OpenTextFile(Application.StartupPath + "\\Products.html",
IOMode.ForWriting, true, Tristate.TristateUseDefault);
            txtstream.WriteLine("<html>");
            txtstream.WriteLine("<head>");
            txtstream.WriteLine("<META http-equiv=\"Content-
Type\" content=\"text/html\">");
            txtstream.WriteLine("<META http-equiv=\"Content-
Type\" contect=\"text/html;charset=UTF-8\"/>");
            txtstream.WriteLine("<title>Products</title>");
            txtstream.WriteLine("</head>");
            txtstream.WriteLine("<body bgcolor='buttonface'>");
            txtstream.WriteLine("<object ID=\"rs\"
classid=\"CLSID:00000535-0000-0010-8000-00AA006D2EA4\" height=0
width=0></object>");
            txtstream.WriteLine("<object ID=\"MSFlexgrid1\"
CLASSID=\"CLSID:6262D3A0-531B-11CF-91F6-C2863C385E30\" height=915
width=1140></OBJECT>");
            txtstream.WriteLine("<script
language=\"javascript\">");
            txtstream.WriteLine("");
            txtstream.WriteLine("rs.ActiveConnection =
\"Provider=Microsoft.Jet.OleDb.4.0;Data Source =
C:\\\\NWind.mdb;\";");
            txtstream.WriteLine("rs.LockType=3;");
            txtstream.WriteLine("rs.CursorLocation=3;");
            txtstream.WriteLine("rs.Source = \"Select * From
Products\";");
            txtstream.WriteLine("rs.Open();");
            txtstream.WriteLine("");
            txtstream.WriteLine("MSFlexgrid1.Rows =
rs.Fields.Count + 1;");
            txtstream.WriteLine("MSFlexgrid1.Cols =
rs.RecordCount + 1;");
            txtstream.WriteLine("");
            txtstream.WriteLine("for (var x = 0; x <
rs.Fields.Count; x++)");
            txtstream.WriteLine("{");
            txtstream.WriteLine("    MSFlexgrid1.Col = 0;");
            txtstream.WriteLine("    MSFlexgrid1.Row = x + 1;");
            txtstream.WriteLine("    MSFlexgrid1.Text =
rs.Fields(x).Name;");
            txtstream.WriteLine("}");
            txtstream.WriteLine("for (var y = 0; y <
rs.RecordCount; y++)");
```

```
        txtstream.WriteLine("{");
        txtstream.WriteLine("    for (var x = 0; x <
rs.Fields.Count; x++)");
        txtstream.WriteLine("    {");
        txtstream.WriteLine("        MSFlexgrid1.Col = y +
1;");
        txtstream.WriteLine("        MSFlexgrid1.Row = x +
1;");
        txtstream.WriteLine("        MSFlexgrid1.Text =
rs.Fields(x).Value;");
        txtstream.WriteLine("    }");
        txtstream.WriteLine("    rs.MoveNext();");
        txtstream.WriteLine("}");
        txtstream.WriteLine("</script>");
        txtstream.WriteLine("</body>");
        txtstream.WriteLine("</html>");
        txtstream.Close();
        webBrowser1.Navigate(Application.StartupPath +
"\\Products.html");
        }
    }
}
```

Spreadsheet Inside a Web Page

Gets done this way:

```
using System;
using System.Collections.Generic;
using System.ComponentModel;
using System.Data;
using System.Drawing;
using System.Linq;
using System.Text;
using System.Windows.Forms;
using Scripting;
namespace WindowsFormsApplication6
{
    public partial class Form8 : Form
    {
        public Form8()
        {
            InitializeComponent();
        }

        private void button1_Click(object sender, EventArgs e)
        {
            FileSystemObject fso = new FileSystemObject();
            TextStream txtstream =
fso.OpenTextFile(Application.StartupPath + "\\Products.html",
IOMode.ForWriting, true, Tristate.TristateUseDefault);
            txtstream.WriteLine("<html>");
            txtstream.WriteLine("<head>");
            txtstream.WriteLine("<META http-equiv=\"Content-
Type\" content=\"text/html\">");
```

```
            txtstream.WriteLine("<META http-equiv=\"Content-
Type\" contect=\"text/html;charset=UTF-8\"/>");
            txtstream.WriteLine("<title>Products</title>");
            txtstream.WriteLine("</head>");
            txtstream.WriteLine("<body bgcolor='buttonface'>");
            txtstream.WriteLine("<object ID=\"rs\"
classid=\"CLSID:00000535-0000-0010-8000-00AA006D2EA4\" height=0
width=0></object>");
            txtstream.WriteLine("<object ID=\"SpreadSheet1\"
classid=\"CLSID:0002E569-0000-0000-C000-000000000046\" height=915
width=1140></OBJECT>");
            txtstream.WriteLine("<script
language=\"javascript\">");
            txtstream.WriteLine("");
            txtstream.WriteLine("rs.ActiveConnection =
\"Provider=Microsoft.Jet.OleDb.4.0;Data Source =
C:\\\\NWind.mdb;\";");
            txtstream.WriteLine("rs.LockType=3;");
            txtstream.WriteLine("rs.CursorLocation=3;");
            txtstream.WriteLine("rs.Source = \"Select * From
Products\";");
            txtstream.WriteLine("rs.Open();");
            txtstream.WriteLine("");

txtstream.WriteLine("SpreadSheet1.ActiveSheet.Cells.Clear();");
            txtstream.WriteLine("");
            txtstream.WriteLine("for (var x = 0; x <
rs.Fields.Count; x++)");
            txtstream.WriteLine("{");
            txtstream.WriteLine("
SpreadSheet1.ActiveSheet.Cells(1, x + 1)  = rs.Fields(x).Name;");
            txtstream.WriteLine("
SpreadSheet1.ActiveSheet.Cells(2, x + 1) = rs.Fields(x).Value;");
            txtstream.WriteLine("}");
            txtstream.WriteLine("
SpreadSheet1.ActiveSheet.Columns.HorizontalAlignment = -4131;");
            txtstream.WriteLine("
SpreadSheet1.ActiveSheet.Columns.AutoFit();");
            txtstream.WriteLine("</script>");
            txtstream.WriteLine("</body>");
            txtstream.WriteLine("</html>");
            txtstream.Close();
            webBrowser1.Navigate(Application.StartupPath +
"\\Products.html");
        }
```

```csharp
private void button3_Click(object sender, EventArgs e)
{
    FileSystemObject fso = new FileSystemObject();
    TextStream txtstream =
fso.OpenTextFile(Application.StartupPath + "\\Products.html",
IOMode.ForWriting, true, Tristate.TristateUseDefault);
    txtstream.WriteLine("<html>");
    txtstream.WriteLine("<head>");
    txtstream.WriteLine("<META http-equiv=\"Content-
Type\" content=\"text/html\">");
    txtstream.WriteLine("<META http-equiv=\"Content-
Type\" contect=\"text/html;charset=UTF-8\"/>");
    txtstream.WriteLine("<title>Products</title>");
    txtstream.WriteLine("</head>");
    txtstream.WriteLine("<body bgcolor='buttonface'>");
    txtstream.WriteLine("<object ID=\"rs\"
classid=\"CLSID:00000535-0000-0010-8000-00AA006D2EA4\" height=0
width=0></object>");
    txtstream.WriteLine("<object ID=\"SpreadSheet1\"
classid=\"CLSID:0002E569-0000-0000-C000-000000000046\" height=915
width=1140></OBJECT>");
    txtstream.WriteLine("<script
language=\"javascript\">");
    txtstream.WriteLine("");
    txtstream.WriteLine("rs.ActiveConnection =
\"Provider=Microsoft.Jet.OleDb.4.0;Data Source =
C:\\\\NWind.mdb;\";");
    txtstream.WriteLine("rs.LockType=3;");
    txtstream.WriteLine("rs.CursorLocation=3;");
    txtstream.WriteLine("rs.Source = \"Select * From
Products\";");
    txtstream.WriteLine("rs.Open();");
    txtstream.WriteLine("");

txtstream.WriteLine("SpreadSheet1.ActiveSheet.Cells.Clear();");
    txtstream.WriteLine("");
    txtstream.WriteLine("for (var x = 0; x <
rs.Fields.Count; x++)");
    txtstream.WriteLine("{");
    txtstream.WriteLine("
SpreadSheet1.ActiveSheet.Cells(x + 1, 1)  = rs.Fields(x).Name;");
    txtstream.WriteLine("
SpreadSheet1.ActiveSheet.Cells(x + 1, 2) = rs.Fields(x).Value;");
    txtstream.WriteLine("}");
```

```csharp
            txtstream.WriteLine("
SpreadSheet1.ActiveSheet.Columns.HorizontalAlignment = -4131;");
            txtstream.WriteLine("
SpreadSheet1.ActiveSheet.Columns.AutoFit();");
            txtstream.WriteLine("</script>");
            txtstream.WriteLine("</body>");
            txtstream.WriteLine("</html>");
            txtstream.Close();
            webBrowser1.Navigate(Application.StartupPath +
"\\Products.html");
        }

        private void button2_Click(object sender, EventArgs e)
        {
            FileSystemObject fso = new FileSystemObject();
            TextStream txtstream =
fso.OpenTextFile(Application.StartupPath + "\\Products.html",
IOMode.ForWriting, true, Tristate.TristateUseDefault);
            txtstream.WriteLine("<html>");
            txtstream.WriteLine("<head>");
            txtstream.WriteLine("<META http-equiv=\"Content-
Type\" content=\"text/html\">");
            txtstream.WriteLine("<META http-equiv=\"Content-
Type\" contect=\"text/html;charset=UTF-8\"/>");
            txtstream.WriteLine("<title>Products</title>");
            txtstream.WriteLine("</head>");
            txtstream.WriteLine("<body bgcolor='buttonface'>");
            txtstream.WriteLine("<object ID=\"rs\"
classid=\"CLSID:00000535-0000-0010-8000-00AA006D2EA4\" height=0
width=0></object>");
            txtstream.WriteLine("<object ID=\"SpreadSheet1\"
classid=\"CLSID:0002E569-0000-0000-C000-000000000046\" height=915
width=1140></OBJECT>");
            txtstream.WriteLine("<script
language=\"javascript\">");
            txtstream.WriteLine("");
            txtstream.WriteLine("rs.ActiveConnection =
\"Provider=Microsoft.Jet.OleDb.4.0;Data Source =
C:\\\\\NWind.mdb;\";");
            txtstream.WriteLine("rs.LockType=3;");
            txtstream.WriteLine("rs.CursorLocation=3;");
            txtstream.WriteLine("rs.Source = \"Select * From
Products\";");
            txtstream.WriteLine("rs.Open();");
            txtstream.WriteLine("");
```

```
txtstream.WriteLine("SpreadSheet1.ActiveSheet.Cells.Clear();");
        txtstream.WriteLine("");
        txtstream.WriteLine("rs.MoveFirst();");
        txtstream.WriteLine("for (var x = 0; x <
rs.Fields.Count; x++)");
        txtstream.WriteLine("{");
        txtstream.WriteLine("
SpreadSheet1.ActiveSheet.Cells(1, x + 1)  = rs.Fields(x).Name;");
        txtstream.WriteLine("}");
        txtstream.WriteLine("for (var y = 0; y <
rs.RecordCount; y++)");
        txtstream.WriteLine("{");
        txtstream.WriteLine("    for (var x = 0; x <
rs.Fields.Count; x++)");
        txtstream.WriteLine("    {");
        txtstream.WriteLine("
SpreadSheet1.ActiveSheet.Cells(y+2, x + 1)  =
rs.Fields(x).Value;");
        txtstream.WriteLine("    }");
        txtstream.WriteLine("    rs.MoveNext();");
        txtstream.WriteLine("}");
        txtstream.WriteLine("
SpreadSheet1.ActiveSheet.Columns.HorizontalAlignment = -4131;");
        txtstream.WriteLine("
SpreadSheet1.ActiveSheet.Columns.AutoFit();");
        txtstream.WriteLine("</script>");
        txtstream.WriteLine("</body>");
        txtstream.WriteLine("</html>");
        txtstream.Close();
        webBrowser1.Navigate(Application.StartupPath +
"\\Products.html");
    }

    private void button4_Click(object sender, EventArgs e)
    {
        FileSystemObject fso = new FileSystemObject();
        TextStream txtstream =
fso.OpenTextFile(Application.StartupPath + "\\Products.html",
IOMode.ForWriting, true, Tristate.TristateUseDefault);
        txtstream.WriteLine("<html>");
        txtstream.WriteLine("<head>");
        txtstream.WriteLine("<META http-equiv=\"Content-
Type\" content=\"text/html\">");
```

```
            txtstream.WriteLine("<META http-equiv=\"Content-
Type\" contect=\"text/html;charset=UTF-8\"/>");
            txtstream.WriteLine("<title>Products</title>");
            txtstream.WriteLine("</head>");
            txtstream.WriteLine("<body bgcolor='buttonface'>");
            txtstream.WriteLine("<object ID=\"rs\"
classid=\"CLSID:00000535-0000-0010-8000-00AA006D2EA4\" height=0
width=0></object>");
            txtstream.WriteLine("<object ID=\"SpreadSheet1\"
classid=\"CLSID:0002E569-0000-0000-C000-000000000046\" height=915
width=1140></OBJECT>");
            txtstream.WriteLine("<script
language=\"javascript\">");
            txtstream.WriteLine("");
            txtstream.WriteLine("rs.ActiveConnection =
\"Provider=Microsoft.Jet.OleDb.4.0;Data Source =
C:\\\\NWind.mdb;\";");
            txtstream.WriteLine("rs.LockType=3;");
            txtstream.WriteLine("rs.CursorLocation=3;");
            txtstream.WriteLine("rs.Source = \"Select * From
Products\";");
            txtstream.WriteLine("rs.Open();");
            txtstream.WriteLine("");

txtstream.WriteLine("SpreadSheet1.ActiveSheet.Cells.Clear();");
            txtstream.WriteLine("");
            txtstream.WriteLine("rs.MoveFirst();");
            txtstream.WriteLine("for (var x = 0; x <
rs.Fields.Count; x++)");
            txtstream.WriteLine("{");
            txtstream.WriteLine("
SpreadSheet1.ActiveSheet.Cells(x + 1, 1)  = rs.Fields(x).Name;");
            txtstream.WriteLine("}");
            txtstream.WriteLine("for (var y = 0; y <
rs.RecordCount; y++)");
            txtstream.WriteLine("{");
            txtstream.WriteLine("    for (var x = 0; x <
rs.Fields.Count; x++)");
            txtstream.WriteLine("    {");
            txtstream.WriteLine("
SpreadSheet1.ActiveSheet.Cells(x + 1, y + 2)  =
rs.Fields(x).Value;");
            txtstream.WriteLine("    }");
            txtstream.WriteLine("    rs.MoveNext();");
            txtstream.WriteLine("}");
```

```
            txtstream.WriteLine("
SpreadSheet1.ActiveSheet.Columns.HorizontalAlignment = -4131;");
            txtstream.WriteLine("
SpreadSheet1.ActiveSheet.Columns.AutoFit();");
            txtstream.WriteLine("</script>");
            txtstream.WriteLine("</body>");
            txtstream.WriteLine("</html>");
            txtstream.Close();
            webBrowser1.Navigate(Application.StartupPath +
"\\Products.html");
        }

        private void splitContainer1_Panel1_Paint(object sender,
PaintEventArgs e)
        {

        }
    }
}
```

Okay, so what's the difference between HTML written now, written interactively, and at runtime?

Written now, means the program writes the html as a product of a recordset that is called at the time the program runs. Written interactively means the code statically designs the way the html will look but uses the same connection string and query inside the html to use the freshest data. Written at runtime, uses the host, in this case the C# IDE, to write out the entire html so that nothing is done in the IDE but to add the connection string and query and to perform that task of creating the file, writing it out in a text file.

Below are examples of all three:

Written now

```
        public void
write_single_line_horizontal_code_written_now(string cnstr,
string strQuery)
        {
```

```csharp
            FileSystemObject fso = new FileSystemObject();
            TextStream txtstream =
fso.OpenTextFile(Application.StartupPath + "\\Products.html",
IOMode.ForWriting, true, Tristate.TristateUseDefault);
            txtstream.WriteLine("<html>");
            txtstream.WriteLine("<head>");
            txtstream.WriteLine("<title>products</title>");
            txtstream.WriteLine("</head>");
            txtstream.WriteLine("<body>");
            txtstream.WriteLine("<table>");
            txtstream.WriteLine("<tr>");
            ADODB.Recordset rs = new ADODB.Recordset();
            rs.let_ActiveConnection(cnstr);
            rs.LockType = LockTypeEnum.adLockOptimistic;
            rs.CursorLocation = CursorLocationEnum.adUseClient;
            rs.let_Source(strQuery);
            rs.Open();
            for(int x=0; x < rs.Fields.Count; x++)
            {
                txtstream.WriteLine("<th>" + rs.Fields[x].Name
+"</th>");
            }
            txtstream.WriteLine("<tr>");
            for(int x=0; x < rs.Fields.Count; x++)
            {
                txtstream.WriteLine("<td>" + rs.Fields[x].Value
+"</td>" );
            }
            txtstream.WriteLine("</tr>");
            txtstream.WriteLine("</table>");
            txtstream.WriteLine("</body>");
            txtstream.WriteLine("</html>");
            txtstream. Close();

}
```

Written Interactively

```csharp
        public void
write_single_line_horizontal_code_written_Interactively(string
cnstr, string strQuery)
        {
            cnstr = cnstr.Replace("\\", "\\\\");
```

```csharp
            FileSystemObject fso = new FileSystemObject();
            TextStream txtstream =
fso.OpenTextFile(Application.StartupPath + "\\Products.html",
IOMode.ForWriting, true, Tristate.TristateUseDefault);
            txtstream.WriteLine("<html>");
            txtstream.WriteLine("<head>");
            txtstream.WriteLine("<title>products</title>");
            txtstream.WriteLine("<object ID=\"rs\"
classid=\"CLSID:00000535-0000-0010-8000-00AA006D2EA4\" height=0
width=0></object>");
            txtstream.WriteLine("<script
language=\"javascript\">");
            txtstream.WriteLine("");
            txtstream.WriteLine("rs.ActiveConnection = \"" +
cnstr + "\";");
            txtstream.WriteLine("rs.LockType=3;");
            txtstream.WriteLine("rs.CursorLocation=3;");
            txtstream.WriteLine("rs.Source = \"" + strQuery +
"\";");
            txtstream.WriteLine("rs.Open();");
            txtstream.WriteLine("</script>");
            txtstream.WriteLine("");
            txtstream.WriteLine("</head>");
            txtstream.WriteLine("<body>");
            txtstream.WriteLine("<table>");

            ADODB.Recordset rs = new ADODB.Recordset();

rs.let_ActiveConnection("Provider=Microsoft.Jet.OleDb.4.0;Data
Source = C:\\NWind.mdb;");
            rs.LockType = LockTypeEnum.adLockOptimistic;
            rs.CursorLocation = CursorLocationEnum.adUseClient;
            rs.let_Source("Select * From Products");
            rs.Open();

            txtstream.WriteLine("<tr>");
            for(int x=0; x < rs.Fields.Count; x++)
            {
                txtstream.WriteLine("<th>" + rs.Fields[x].Name +
"</th>");
            }
            txtstream.WriteLine("</tr>");
            txtstream.WriteLine("<tr>");
            txtstream.WriteLine("<script
language=\"javascript\">");
```

```
            txtstream.WriteLine("for(var x=0; x <
rs.Fields.Count; x++)");
            txtstream.WriteLine("{");
            txtstream.WriteLine("document.writeln(\"<td>\" +
rs.Fields(x).Value + \"</td>\");");
            txtstream.WriteLine("}");
            txtstream.WriteLine("document.writeln(\"</tr>\");");
            txtstream.WriteLine("</script>");
            txtstream.WriteLine("</tr>");
            txtstream.WriteLine("</table>");
            txtstream.WriteLine("</body>");
            txtstream.WriteLine("</html>");
            txtstream. Close();

        }
```

Written At Runtime

```
        public void
write_single_line_horizontal_code_written_At_Runtine(string
cnstr, string strQuery)
        {
            cnstr = cnstr.Replace("\\", "\\\\");

            FileSystemObject fso = new FileSystemObject();
            TextStream txtstream =
fso.OpenTextFile(Application.StartupPath + "\\Products.html",
IOMode.ForWriting, true, Tristate.TristateUseDefault);
            txtstream.WriteLine("<html>");
            txtstream.WriteLine("<head>");
            txtstream.WriteLine("<title>products</title>");
            txtstream.WriteLine("<object ID=\"rs\"
classid=\"CLSID:00000535-0000-0010-8000-00AA006D2EA4\" height=0
width=0></object>");
            txtstream.WriteLine("");
            txtstream.WriteLine("</head>");
            txtstream.WriteLine("<body>");
            txtstream.WriteLine("<script
language=\"javascript\">");
            txtstream.WriteLine("");
            txtstream.WriteLine("rs.ActiveConnection = \"" +
cnstr + "\";");
            txtstream.WriteLine("rs.LockType=3;");
```

```
            txtstream.WriteLine("rs.CursorLocation=3;");
            txtstream.WriteLine("rs.Source = \"" + strQuery +
"\";");
            txtstream.WriteLine("rs.Open();");

txtstream.WriteLine("document.writeln(\"<table>\");");
            txtstream.WriteLine("document.writeln(\"<tr>\");");
            txtstream.WriteLine("for(var x=0; x <
rs.Fields.Count; x++)");
            txtstream.WriteLine("{");
                txtstream.WriteLine("document.writeln(\"<th>\" +
rs.Fields(x).Name + \"</th>\");");
            txtstream.WriteLine("}");
            txtstream.WriteLine("document.writeln(\"</tr>\");");
            txtstream.WriteLine("document.writeln(\"<tr>\");");
            txtstream.WriteLine("for(var x=0; x <
rs.Fields.Count; x++)");
            txtstream.WriteLine("{");
                txtstream.WriteLine("document.writeln(\"<td>\" +
rs.Fields(x).Value + \"</td>\");");
            txtstream.WriteLine("}");
            txtstream.WriteLine("document.writeln(\"</tr>\");");

txtstream.WriteLine("document.writeln(\"</table>\");");
            txtstream.WriteLine("</script>");
            txtstream.WriteLine("</body>");
            txtstream.WriteLine("</html>");
            txtstream. Close();

        }
```

And there you have to code to see for yourself how each is slightly different than the other.

There is also the notion of being bound, cloaked, dynamic or static. While bound is a form of being static – also written now – static also enables us to do more with the logic. Bound can either be multi-line or single-line Horizontal, Static can be written to render the information in multi-line or single-line Horizontal and multi-line or single-line Vertical.

Bound HTML

Bound code must be either interactive or at runtime. Simply put, there needs to be active code inside the browser itself to work...wrong. Watch this:

Below is the single-line Horizontal Code:

```
using System;
using System.Collections.Generic;
using System.ComponentModel;
using System.Data;
using System.Drawing;
using System.Linq;
using System.Text;
using System.Windows.Forms;
using ADODB;
using Scripting;
using mshtml;

namespace insideout
{
    public partial class Form1 : Form
    {
        public Form1()
        {
            InitializeComponent();
        }
        String cnstr = "Provider=Microsoft.Jet.OleDb.4.0;Data
Source = C:\\NWind.mdb;";
        string strQuery = "Select * from Products";

        private void Form1_Load(object sender, EventArgs e)
```

```
{
        ADODB.Recordset rs = new ADODB.Recordset();
        rs.let_ActiveConnection(cnstr);
        rs.CursorLocation = CursorLocationEnum.adUseClient;
        rs.LockType = LockTypeEnum.adLockOptimistic;
        rs.let_Source(strQuery);
        rs.Open();



        cnstr = cnstr.Replace("\\", "\\\\");

        FileSystemObject fso = new FileSystemObject();
        TextStream txtstream =
fso.OpenTextFile(Application.StartupPath + "\\Products.html",
IOMode.ForWriting, true, Tristate.TristateUseDefault);
        txtstream.WriteLine("<html>");
        txtstream.WriteLine("<head>");
        txtstream.WriteLine("<title>products</title>");
        txtstream.WriteLine("<object ID=\"rs\"
classid=\"CLSID:00000535-0000-0010-8000-00AA006D2EA4\" height=0
width=0></object>");
        txtstream.WriteLine("");
        txtstream.WriteLine("</head>");
        txtstream.WriteLine("<body>");
        txtstream.WriteLine("<script
language=\"javascript\">");
        txtstream.WriteLine("");
        txtstream.WriteLine("rs.ActiveConnection = \"" +
cnstr + "\";");
        txtstream.WriteLine("rs.LockType=3;");
        txtstream.WriteLine("rs.CursorLocation=3;");
        txtstream.WriteLine("rs.Source = \"" + strQuery +
"\";");
        txtstream.WriteLine("rs.Open();");
        txtstream.WriteLine("");
        txtstream.WriteLine("document.writeln(\"<table
datasrc=#rs>\")");

txtstream.WriteLine("document.writeln(\"<thead><tr>\")");
        txtstream.WriteLine("for (var x = 0; x <
rs.Fields.Count; x++)");
        txtstream.WriteLine("{");
```

```
            txtstream.WriteLine("      document.writeln(\"<th>\" +
rs.Fields[x].Name + \"</th>\");");
            txtstream.WriteLine("}");

txtstream.WriteLine("document.writeln(\"</tr></thead>\");");

txtstream.WriteLine("document.writeln(\"<tbody><tr>\");");
            txtstream.WriteLine("for (var x = 0; x <
rs.Fields.Count; x++)");
            txtstream.WriteLine("{");
            txtstream.WriteLine("      document.writeln(\"<td><span
datasrc=#rs datafld=\" + rs.Fields[x].Name + \"></span></td>\");");
            txtstream.WriteLine("}");

txtstream.WriteLine("document.writeln(\"</tr></tbody>\");");

txtstream.WriteLine("document.writeln(\"</table>\");");
            txtstream.WriteLine("</script>");
            txtstream.WriteLine("</body>");
            txtstream.WriteLine("</html>");
            txtstream.Close();

            webBrowser1.Navigate(Application.StartupPath +
"\\Products.html");

        }

    }

}
```

Here's the output:

```
<html>
<head>
<title>products</title>
<object id="rs" classid="CLSID:00000535-0000-0010-8000-00AA006D2EA4"
height=0 width=0></object>
</head>
<body>
<script language="javascript">
```

```
rs.ActiveConnection    =    "Provider=Microsoft.Jet.OleDb.4.0;Data    Source    =
C:\\NWind.mdb;";
rs.CursorLocation=3;
rs.LockType=3;
rs.Source = "Select * from Products";
rs.Open();
</script>
<table>
<thead><tr>
<th>ProductID</th>
<th>ProductName</th>
<th>SupplierID</th>
<th>CategoryID</th>
<th>QuantityPerUnit</th>
<th>UnitPrice</th>
<th>UnitsInStock</th>
<th>UnitsOnOrder</th>
<th>ReorderLevel</th>
<th>Discontinued</th>
</tr></thead>
<tbody><tr>
<td><span datasrc=#rs datafld="ProductID"></span></td>
<td><span datasrc=#rs datafld="ProductName"></span></span></td>
<td><span datasrc=#rs datafld="SupplierID"></span></td>
<td><span datasrc=#rs datafld="CategoryID"></span></td>
<td><span datasrc=#rs datafld="QuantityPerUnit"></span></td>
<td><span datasrc=#rs datafld="UnitPrice"></span></td>
<td><span datasrc=#rs datafld="UnitsInStock"></span></td>
<td><span datasrc=#rs datafld="UnitsOnOrder"></span></td>
<td><span datasrc=#rs datafld="ReorderLevel"></span></td>
<td><span datasrc=#rs datafld="Discontinued"></span></td>
</tr></tbody>
</table>
```

```
    </body>
    </html>
```

Here's the Multi-line Horizontal Code:

```csharp
using System;
using System.Collections.Generic;
using System.ComponentModel;
using System.Data;
using System.Drawing;
using System.Linq;
using System.Text;
using System.Windows.Forms;
using ADODB;
using Scripting;
using mshtml;

namespace insideout
{
    public partial class Form1 : Form
    {
        public Form1()
        {
            InitializeComponent();
        }
        String cnstr = "Provider=Microsoft.Jet.OleDb.4.0;Data
Source = C:\\NWind.mdb;";
        string strQuery = "Select * from Products";

        private void Form1_Load(object sender, EventArgs e)
        {

            ADODB.Recordset rs = new ADODB.Recordset();
            rs.let_ActiveConnection(cnstr);
            rs.CursorLocation = CursorLocationEnum.adUseClient;
            rs.LockType = LockTypeEnum.adLockOptimistic;
            rs.let_Source(strQuery);
            rs.Open();


            cnstr = cnstr.Replace("\\", "\\\\");
```

```csharp
            FileSystemObject fso = new FileSystemObject();
            TextStream txtstream =
fso.OpenTextFile(Application.StartupPath + "\\Products.html",
IOMode.ForWriting, true, Tristate.TristateUseDefault);
            txtstream.WriteLine("<html>");
            txtstream.WriteLine("<head>");
            txtstream.WriteLine("<title>products</title>");
            txtstream.WriteLine("<object ID=\"rs\"
classid=\"CLSID:00000535-0000-0010-8000-00AA006D2EA4\" height=0
width=0></object>");
            txtstream.WriteLine("");
            txtstream.WriteLine("</head>");
            txtstream.WriteLine("<body>");
            txtstream.WriteLine("<script
language=\"javascript\">");
            txtstream.WriteLine("");
            txtstream.WriteLine("rs.ActiveConnection = \"" +
cnstr + "\";");
            txtstream.WriteLine("rs.LockType=3;");
            txtstream.WriteLine("rs.CursorLocation=3;");
            txtstream.WriteLine("rs.Source = \"" + strQuery +
"\";");
            txtstream.WriteLine("rs.Open();");
            txtstream.WriteLine("");
            txtstream.WriteLine("document.writeln(\"<table
datasrc=#rs>\")");

txtstream.WriteLine("document.writeln(\"<thead><tr>\")");
            txtstream.WriteLine("for (var x = 0; x <
rs.Fields.Count; x++)");
            txtstream.WriteLine("{");
            txtstream.WriteLine("    document.writeln(\"<th>\" +
rs.Fields[x].Name + \"</th>\");");
            txtstream.WriteLine("}");

txtstream.WriteLine("document.writeln(\"</tr></thead>\");");

txtstream.WriteLine("document.writeln(\"<tbody><tr>\");");
            txtstream.WriteLine("for (var x = 0; x <
rs.Fields.Count; x++)");
            txtstream.WriteLine("{");
            txtstream.WriteLine("    document.writeln(\"<td><span
datafld=\" + rs.Fields[x].Name + \"></span></td>\");");
            txtstream.WriteLine("}");
```

```
txtstream.WriteLine("document.writeln(\"</tr></tbody>\");");

txtstream.WriteLine("document.writeln(\"</table>\");");
            txtstream.WriteLine("</script>");
            txtstream.WriteLine("</body>");
            txtstream.WriteLine("</html>");
            txtstream.Close();

            webBrowser1.Navigate(Application.StartupPath +
"\\Products.html");

        }


    }

}
```

Here's the output:


```
<html>
<head>
<title>products</title>
<object id="rs" classid="CLSID:00000535-0000-0010-8000-00AA006D2EA4"
height=0 width=0></object>
</head>
<body>
<script language="javascript">
rs.ActiveConnection  =  "Provider=Microsoft.Jet.OleDb.4.0;Data   Source  =
C:\\NWind.mdb;";
rs.CursorLocation=3;
rs.LockType=3;
rs.Source = "Select * from Products";
```

```
rs.Open();
</script>
<table datasrc=#rs >
<thead><tr>
<th>ProductID</th>
<th>ProductName</th>
<th>SupplierID</th>
<th>CategoryID</th>
<th>QuantityPerUnit</th>
<th>UnitPrice</th>
<th>UnitsInStock</th>
<th>UnitsOnOrder</th>
<th>ReorderLevel</th>
<th>Discontinued</th>
</tr></thead>
<tbody><tr>
<td><span datafld="ProductID"></span></td>
<td><span datafld="ProductName"></span></span></td>
<td><span datafld="SupplierID"></span></td>
<td><span datafld="CategoryID"></span></td>
<td><span datafld="QuantityPerUnit"></span></td>
<td><span datafld="UnitPrice"></span></td>
<td><span datafld="UnitsInStock"></span></td>
<td><span datafld="UnitsOnOrder"></span></td>
<td><span datafld="ReorderLevel"></span></td>
<td><span datafld="Discontinued"></span></td>
</tr></tbody>
</table>
</body>
</html>
```

Cloaked HTML

What you get was not what you see

I love this one. Let's take a look at the code.

```csharp
public void
write_single_line_horizontal_code_written_At_Runtine(string
cnstr, string strQuery)
    {
        cnstr = cnstr.Replace("\\", "\\\\");

        FileSystemObject fso = new FileSystemObject();
        TextStream txtstream =
fso.OpenTextFile(Application.StartupPath + "\\Products.html",
IOMode.ForWriting, true, Tristate.TristateUseDefault);
        txtstream.WriteLine("<html>");
        txtstream.WriteLine("<head>");
        txtstream.WriteLine("<title>products</title>");
        txtstream.WriteLine("<object ID=\"rs\"
classid=\"CLSID:00000535-0000-0010-8000-00AA006D2EA4\" height=0
width=0></object>");
        txtstream.WriteLine("");
        txtstream.WriteLine("</head>");
        txtstream.WriteLine("<body onload=\"start()\">");
        txtstream.WriteLine("<script
language=\"javascript\">");
        txtstream.WriteLine("");
        txtstream.WriteLine("rs.ActiveConnection = \"" +
cnstr + "\";");
        txtstream.WriteLine("rs.LockType=3;");
        txtstream.WriteLine("rs.CursorLocation=3;");
        txtstream.WriteLine("rs.Source = \"" + strQuery +
"\";");
```

```
txtstream.WriteLine("rs.Open();");
txtstream.WriteLine("");
txtstream.WriteLine("var mystr=\"\";");
txtstream.WriteLine("");
txtstream.WriteLine(" function start()");
txtstream.WriteLine(" {");
txtstream.WriteLine("");
txtstream.WriteLine("    mystr= '<table>\\r';");
txtstream.WriteLine("    mystr = mystr +
'<tr>\\r';");
txtstream.WriteLine("    for(var x=0; x <
rs.Fields.Count; x++)");
txtstream.WriteLine("    {");
txtstream.WriteLine("      mystr =  mystr + '<th>'
+ rs.Fields(x).Name + '</th>\\r';");
txtstream.WriteLine("    }");
txtstream.WriteLine("    mystr =  mystr +
'</tr>\\r';");
txtstream.WriteLine("    mystr =  mystr +
'<tr>\\r';");
txtstream.WriteLine("    for(var x=0; x <
rs.Fields.Count; x++)");
txtstream.WriteLine("    {");
txtstream.WriteLine("      mystr =  mystr + '<td>'
+ rs.Fields(x).Value + '</td>\\r';");
txtstream.WriteLine("    }");
txtstream.WriteLine("    mystr =  mystr +
'</tr>\\r';");
txtstream.WriteLine("    mystr =  mystr +
'</table>\\r';");
txtstream.WriteLine("    document.writeln(mystr);");
txtstream.WriteLine("}");
txtstream.WriteLine("</script>");
txtstream.WriteLine("</body>");
txtstream.WriteLine("</html>");
txtstream. Close();

}
```

And The File:

```html
<html>
<head>
<title>products</title>
<object ID="rs" classid="CLSID:00000535-0000-0010-8000-00AA006D2EA4"
height=0 width=0></object>

</head>
<body onload="start()">
<script language="javascript">

rs.ActiveConnection = "Provider=Microsoft.Jet.OleDb.4.0;Data Source =
C:\\NWind.mdb;";
rs.LockType=3;
rs.CursorLocation=3;
rs.Source = "Select * From Products";
rs.Open();

var mystr="";

function start()
{

    mystr= '<table>\r';
    mystr = mystr + '<tr>\r';
    for(var x=0; x < rs.Fields.Count; x++)
    {
        mystr = mystr + '<th>' + rs.Fields(x).Name + '</th>\r';
    }
    mystr = mystr + '</tr>\r';
    mystr = mystr + '<tr>\r';
```

```
    for(var x=0; x < rs.Fields.Count; x++)
    {
       mystr =  mystr + '<td>' + rs.Fields(x).Value + '</td>\r';
    }
    mystr =  mystr + '</tr>\r';
    mystr =  mystr + '</table>\r';
    document.writeln(mystr);
}
</script>
</body>
</html>
```

And the view:

ProductID	ProductName	SupplierID	CategoryID	QuantityPerUnit	UnitPrice	UnitsInStock	UnitsOnOrder	ReorderLevel	Discontinued
1	Chai	1	1	10 boxes x 20 bags	18	39	0	10	false

And when you view the source:

```
<table>
<tr>
<th>ProductID</th>
<th>ProductName</th>
<th>SupplierID</th>
<th>CategoryID</th>
<th>QuantityPerUnit</th>
<th>UnitPrice</th>
<th>UnitsInStock</th>
<th>UnitsOnOrder</th>
<th>ReorderLevel</th>
<th>Discontinued</th>
```

```
</tr>
<tr>
<td>1</td>
<td>Chai</td>
<td>1</td>
<td>1</td>
<td>10 boxes x 20 bags</td>
<td>18</td>
<td>39</td>
<td>0</td>
<td>10</td>
<td>false</td>
</tr>
</table>
```

Which is why I call it cloaked.

Dynamic HTML

Dynamically driven HTML doesn't look much different than cloaked. Below, is an example of what is meant:

```csharp
using System;
using System.Collections.Generic;
using System.ComponentModel;
using System.Data;
using System.Drawing;
using System.Linq;
using System.Text;
using System.Windows.Forms;
using ADODB;
using Scripting;
using mshtml;

namespace insideout
{
    public partial class Form1 : Form
    {
        public Form1()
        {
            InitializeComponent();
        }
        String cnstr = "Provider=Microsoft.Jet.OleDb.4.0;Data
Source = C:\\NWind.mdb;";
        string strQuery = "Select * from Products";

        private void Form1_Load(object sender, EventArgs e)
        {
```

```csharp
ADODB.Recordset rs = new ADODB.Recordset();
rs.let_ActiveConnection(cnstr);
rs.CursorLocation = CursorLocationEnum.adUseClient;
rs.LockType = LockTypeEnum.adLockOptimistic;
rs.let_Source(strQuery);
rs.Open();



cnstr = cnstr.Replace("\\", "\\\\");

FileSystemObject fso = new FileSystemObject();
TextStream txtstream =
fso.OpenTextFile(Application.StartupPath + "\\Products.html",
IOMode.ForWriting, true, Tristate.TristateUseDefault);
txtstream.WriteLine("<html>");
txtstream.WriteLine("<head>");
txtstream.WriteLine("<title>products</title>");
txtstream.WriteLine("<object ID=\"rs\"
classid=\"CLSID:00000535-0000-0010-8000-00AA006D2EA4\" height=0
width=0></object>");
txtstream.WriteLine("");
txtstream.WriteLine("</head>");
txtstream.WriteLine("<body>");
txtstream.WriteLine("<script
language=\"javascript\">");
txtstream.WriteLine("");
txtstream.WriteLine("rs.ActiveConnection = \"" +
cnstr + "\";");
txtstream.WriteLine("rs.LockType=3;");
txtstream.WriteLine("rs.CursorLocation=3;");
txtstream.WriteLine("rs.Source = \"" + strQuery +
"\";");
txtstream.WriteLine("rs.Open();");
txtstream.WriteLine("");
txtstream.WriteLine("document.writeln(\"<table>\")");
txtstream.WriteLine("document.writeln(\"<tr>\")");
txtstream.WriteLine("for (var x = 0; x <
rs.Fields.Count; x++)");
txtstream.WriteLine("{");
txtstream.WriteLine("   document.writeln(\"<th>\" +
rs.Fields[x].Name + \"</th>\");");
txtstream.WriteLine("}");
txtstream.WriteLine("document.writeln(\"</tr>\");");
txtstream.WriteLine("document.writeln(\"<tr>\");");
```

```
            txtstream.WriteLine("for (var x = 0; x <
rs.Fields.Count; x++)");
            txtstream.WriteLine("{");
            txtstream.WriteLine("    document.writeln(\"<td>\" +
rs.Fields[x].Name + \"</td>\");");
            txtstream.WriteLine("}");
            txtstream.WriteLine("document.writeln(\"</tr>\");");

txtstream.WriteLine("document.writeln(\"</table>\");");
            txtstream.WriteLine("</script>");
            txtstream.WriteLine("</body>");
            txtstream.WriteLine("</html>");
            txtstream.Close();

            webBrowser1.Navigate(Application.StartupPath +
"\\Products.html");

        }

    }

}
```

The output looks like this:

```
<html>
<head>
<title>products</title>
<object    ID="rs"    classid="CLSID:00000535-0000-0010-8000-00AA006D2EA4"
height=0 width=0></object>

</head>
<body>
<script language="javascript">

rs.ActiveConnection   =   "Provider=Microsoft.Jet.OleDb.4.0;Data   Source   =
C:\\NWind.mdb;";
rs.LockType=3;
rs.CursorLocation=3;
```

```
rs.Source = "Select * from Products";
rs.Open();

document.writeln("<table>")
document.writeln("<tr>")
for (var x = 0; x < rs.Fields.Count; x++)
{
    document.writeln("<th>" + rs.Fields(x).Name + "</th>");
}
document.writeln("</tr>");
document.writeln("<tr>");
for (var x = 0; x < rs.Fields.Count; x++)
{
    document.writeln("<td>" + rs.Fields(x).Value + "</td>");
}
document.writeln("</tr>");
document.writeln("</table>");
</script>
</body>
</html>
```

The multi-line Horizontal code looks like this:

```
using System;
using System.Collections.Generic;
using System.ComponentModel;
using System.Data;
using System.Drawing;
using System.Linq;
using System.Text;
using System.Windows.Forms;
using ADODB;
using Scripting;
using mshtml;

namespace insideout
{
```

```csharp
public partial class Form1 : Form
{
    public Form1()
    {
        InitializeComponent();
    }
    String cnstr = "Provider=Microsoft.Jet.OleDb.4.0;Data
Source = C:\\NWind.mdb;";
    string strQuery = "Select * from Products";

    private void Form1_Load(object sender, EventArgs e)
    {

        ADODB.Recordset rs = new ADODB.Recordset();
        rs.let_ActiveConnection(cnstr);
        rs.CursorLocation = CursorLocationEnum.adUseClient;
        rs.LockType = LockTypeEnum.adLockOptimistic;
        rs.let_Source(strQuery);
        rs.Open();



        cnstr = cnstr.Replace("\\", "\\\\");

        FileSystemObject fso = new FileSystemObject();
        TextStream txtstream =
fso.OpenTextFile(Application.StartupPath + "\\Products.html",
IOMode.ForWriting, true, Tristate.TristateUseDefault);
        txtstream.WriteLine("<html>");
        txtstream.WriteLine("<head>");
        txtstream.WriteLine("<title>products</title>");
        txtstream.WriteLine("<object ID=\"rs\"
classid=\"CLSID:00000535-0000-0010-8000-00AA006D2EA4\" height=0
width=0></object>");
        txtstream.WriteLine("");
        txtstream.WriteLine("</head>");
        txtstream.WriteLine("<body>");
        txtstream.WriteLine("<script
language=\"javascript\">");
        txtstream.WriteLine("");
        txtstream.WriteLine("rs.ActiveConnection = \"" +
cnstr + "\";");
        txtstream.WriteLine("rs.LockType=3;");
        txtstream.WriteLine("rs.CursorLocation=3;");
```

```csharp
            txtstream.WriteLine("rs.Source = \"" + strQuery +
"\";");
            txtstream.WriteLine("rs.Open();");
            txtstream.WriteLine("");
            txtstream.WriteLine("document.writeln(\"<table>\")");
            txtstream.WriteLine("document.writeln(\"<tr>\")");
            txtstream.WriteLine("for (var x = 0; x <
rs.Fields.Count; x++)");
            txtstream.WriteLine("{");
            txtstream.WriteLine("    document.writeln(\"<th>\" +
rs.Fields(x).Name + \"</th>\");");
            txtstream.WriteLine("}");
            txtstream.WriteLine("document.writeln(\"</tr>\");");
            txtstream.WriteLine("");
            txtstream.WriteLine("while(rs.eof == false)");
            txtstream.WriteLine("{");
            txtstream.WriteLine("
document.writeln(\"<tr>\");");
            txtstream.WriteLine("    for (var x = 0; x <
rs.Fields.Count; x++)");
            txtstream.WriteLine("    {");
            txtstream.WriteLine("
document.writeln(\"<td>\" + rs.Fields(x).Value + \"</td>\");");
            txtstream.WriteLine("    }");
            txtstream.WriteLine("
document.writeln(\"</tr>\");");
            txtstream.WriteLine("    rs.MoveNext();");
            txtstream.WriteLine("}");

txtstream.WriteLine("document.writeln(\"</table>\");");
            txtstream.WriteLine("</script>");
            txtstream.WriteLine("</body>");
            txtstream.WriteLine("</html>");
            txtstream.Close();

            webBrowser1.Navigate(Application.StartupPath +
"\\Products.html");

        }

    }

}
```

And the output looks like this:

```html
<html>
<head>
<title>products</title>
<object    ID="rs"    classid="CLSID:00000535-0000-0010-8000-00AA006D2EA4"
height=0 width=0></object>

</head>
<body>
<script language="javascript">

rs.ActiveConnection    =    "Provider=Microsoft.Jet.OleDb.4.0;Data    Source    =
C:\\NWind.mdb;";
rs.LockType=3;
rs.CursorLocation=3;
rs.Source = "Select * from Products";
rs.Open();

document.writeln("<table>")
document.writeln("<tr>")
for (var x = 0; x < rs.Fields.Count; x++)
{
   document.writeln("<th>" + rs.Fields(x).Name + "</th>");
}
document.writeln("</tr>");

while(rs.EOF == false)
{
   document.writeln("<tr>");
   for (var x = 0; x < rs.Fields.Count; x++)
   {
      document.writeln("<td>" + rs.Fields(x).Value + "</td>");
   }
   document.writeln("</tr>");
```

```
    rs.MoveNext();
}
document.writeln("</table>");
</script>
</body>
</html>
```

Static HTML

Static html means all of the code to render the HTML is accomplished by the program itself. In this case, it is C#. Below, is the code:

For single line horizontal:

```csharp
using System;
using System.Collections.Generic;
using System.ComponentModel;
using System.Data;
using System.Drawing;
using System.Linq;
using System.Text;
using System.Windows.Forms;
using ADODB;
using Scripting;
using mshtml;

namespace insideout
{
    public partial class Form1 : Form
    {
        public Form1()
        {
            InitializeComponent();
        }
```

```
        String cnstr = "Provider=Microsoft.Jet.OleDb.4.0;Data
Source = C:\\NWind.mdb;";
        string strQuery = "Select * from Products";

        private void Form1_Load(object sender, EventArgs e)
        {
            ADODB.Recordset rs = new ADODB.Recordset();
            rs.let_ActiveConnection(cnstr);
            rs.CursorLocation = CursorLocationEnum.adUseClient;
            rs.LockType = LockTypeEnum.adLockOptimistic;
            rs.let_Source(strQuery);
            rs.Open();


            cnstr = cnstr.Replace("\\", "\\\\");

            FileSystemObject fso = new FileSystemObject();
            TextStream txtstream =
fso.OpenTextFile(Application.StartupPath + "\\Products.html",
IOMode.ForWriting, true, Tristate.TristateUseDefault);
            txtstream.WriteLine("<html>");
            txtstream.WriteLine("<head>");
            txtstream.WriteLine("<title>products</title>");
            txtstream.WriteLine("<object ID=\"rs\"
classid=\"CLSID:00000535-0000-0010-8000-00AA006D2EA4\" height=0
width=0></object>");
            txtstream.WriteLine("");
            txtstream.WriteLine("</head>");
            txtstream.WriteLine("<body>");
            txtstream.WriteLine("");
            txtstream.WriteLine("<table>");
            txtstream.WriteLine("<tr>");
            for (var x = 0; x < rs.Fields.Count; x++)
            {
                txtstream.WriteLine("<th>" + rs.Fields[x].Name +
"</th>");
            }
            txtstream.WriteLine("</tr>");
            txtstream.WriteLine("<tr>");
            for (var x = 0; x < rs.Fields.Count; x++)
            {
                txtstream.WriteLine("<td>" + rs.Fields[x].Value +
"</td>");
```

```
            }
            txtstream.WriteLine("</tr>");
            txtstream.WriteLine("</table>");
            txtstream.WriteLine("</script>");
            txtstream.WriteLine("</body>");
            txtstream.WriteLine("</html>");
            txtstream.Close();

            webBrowser1.Navigate(Application.StartupPath +
"\\Products.html");

        }

    }

}
```

The output:

```
<html>
<head>
<title>products</title>
</head>
<body>
<table>
<tr>
<th>ProductID</th>
<th>ProductName</th>
<th>SupplierID</th>
<th>CategoryID</th>
<th>QuantityPerUnit</th>
<th>UnitPrice</th>
<th>UnitsInStock</th>
<th>UnitsOnOrder</th>
<th>ReorderLevel</th>
<th>Discontinued</th>
</tr>
```

```
<tr>
<td>1</td>
<td>Chai</td>
<td>1</td>
<td>1</td>
<td>10 boxes x 20 bags</td>
<td>18</td>
<td>39</td>
<td>0</td>
<td>10</td>
<td>False</td>
</tr>
</table>
</script>
</body>
```

For Multi-line Horizontal:

```
using System;
using System.Collections.Generic;
using System.ComponentModel;
using System.Data;
using System.Drawing;
using System.Linq;
using System.Text;
using System.Windows.Forms;
using ADODB;
using Scripting;
using mshtml;

namespace insideout
{
    public partial class Form1 : Form
    {
        public Form1()
        {
            InitializeComponent();
        }
```

```csharp
        String cnstr = "Provider=Microsoft.Jet.OleDb.4.0;Data
Source = C:\\NWind.mdb;";
        string strQuery = "Select * from Products";

        private void Form1_Load(object sender, EventArgs e)
        {

            ADODB.Recordset rs = new ADODB.Recordset();
            rs.let_ActiveConnection(cnstr);
            rs.CursorLocation = CursorLocationEnum.adUseClient;
            rs.LockType = LockTypeEnum.adLockOptimistic;
            rs.let_Source(strQuery);
            rs.Open();


            cnstr = cnstr.Replace("\\", "\\\\");

            FileSystemObject fso = new FileSystemObject();
            TextStream txtstream =
fso.OpenTextFile(Application.StartupPath + "\\Products.html",
IOMode.ForWriting, true, Tristate.TristateUseDefault);
            txtstream.WriteLine("<html>");
            txtstream.WriteLine("<head>");
            txtstream.WriteLine("<title>products</title>");
            txtstream.WriteLine("<object ID=\"rs\"
classid=\"CLSID:00000535-0000-0010-8000-00AA006D2EA4\" height=0
width=0></object>");
            txtstream.WriteLine("");
            txtstream.WriteLine("</head>");
            txtstream.WriteLine("<body>");
            txtstream.WriteLine("");
            txtstream.WriteLine("<table>");
            txtstream.WriteLine("<tr>");
            for (var x = 0; x < rs.Fields.Count; x++)
            {
                txtstream.WriteLine("<th>" + rs.Fields[x].Name +
"</th>");
            }
            txtstream.WriteLine("</tr>");

            while(rs.EOF == false)
            {
                txtstream.WriteLine("<tr>");
                for (var x = 0; x < rs.Fields.Count; x++)
                {
```

```
                    txtstream.WriteLine("<td>" +
rs.Fields[x].Value + "</td>");
                }
                txtstream.WriteLine("</tr>");
                rs.MoveNext();
            }
            txtstream.WriteLine("</table>");
            txtstream.WriteLine("</body>");
            txtstream.WriteLine("</html>");
            txtstream.Close();

            webBrowser1.Navigate(Application.StartupPath +
"\\Products.html");

        }

    }

}
```

And the output (shortened for page conservation):

```
<html>
<head>
<title>products</title>
<object ID="rs" classid="CLSID:00000535-0000-0010-8000-00AA006D2EA4"
height=0 width=0></object>

</head>
<body>

<table>
<tr>
<th>ProductID</th>
<th>ProductName</th>
<th>SupplierID</th>
<th>CategoryID</th>
<th>QuantityPerUnit</th>
<th>UnitPrice</th>
<th>UnitsInStock</th>
<th>UnitsOnOrder</th>
<th>ReorderLevel</th>
<th>Discontinued</th>
</tr>
<tr>
<td>1</td>
<td>Chai</td>
```

```html
<td>1</td>
<td>1</td>
<td>10 boxes x 20 bags</td>
<td>18</td>
<td>39</td>
<td>0</td>
<td>10</td>
<td>False</td>
</tr>
<tr>
<td>2</td>
<td>Chang</td>
<td>1</td>
<td>1</td>
<td>24 - 12 oz bottles</td>
<td>19</td>
<td>17</td>
<td>40</td>
<td>25</td>
<td>False</td>
</tr>
<tr>
<td>3</td>
<td>Aniseed Syrup</td>
<td>1</td>
<td>2</td>
<td>12 - 550 ml bottles</td>
<td>10</td>
<td>13</td>
<td>70</td>
<td>25</td>
<td>False</td>
</tr>
<tr>
<td>4</td>
<td>Chef Anton's Cajun Seasoning</td>
<td>2</td>
<td>2</td>
<td>48 - 6 oz jars</td>
<td>22</td>
<td>53</td>
<td>0</td>
<td>0</td>
<td>False</td>
</tr>
</table>
</body>
</html>
```

Stylesheets

Decorating your reports with flair

Below are some stylesheets that I created which I'm hoping you might like and use. But, don't worry I won't be offended if you take and modify to your hearts delight. In fact, please do!

NONE

```
txtstream.WriteLine("<style type='text/css'>")
txtstream.WriteLine("th")
txtstream.WriteLine("{")
txtstream.WriteLine("   COLOR: white;")
txtstream.WriteLine("}")
txtstream.WriteLine("td")
txtstream.WriteLine("{")
txtstream.WriteLine("   COLOR: white;")
txtstream.WriteLine("}")
txtstream.WriteLine("</style>")
```

BLACK AND WHITE TEXT

```
txtstream.WriteLine("<style type='text/css'>")
txtstream.WriteLine("th")
```

```
txtstream.WriteLine("{")
txtstream.WriteLine("    COLOR: white;")
txtstream.WriteLine("    BACKGROUND-COLOR: black;")
txtstream.WriteLine("    FONT-FAMILY:font-family: Cambria, serif;")
txtstream.WriteLine("    FONT-SIZE: 12px;")
txtstream.WriteLine("    text-align: left;")
txtstream.WriteLine("    white-Space: nowrap;")
txtstream.WriteLine("}")
txtstream.WriteLine("td")
txtstream.WriteLine("{")
txtstream.WriteLine("    COLOR: white;")
txtstream.WriteLine("    BACKGROUND-COLOR: black;")
txtstream.WriteLine("    FONT-FAMILY: font-family: Cambria, serif;")
txtstream.WriteLine("    FONT-SIZE: 12px;")
txtstream.WriteLine("    text-align: left;")
txtstream.WriteLine("    white-Space: nowrap;")
txtstream.WriteLine("}")
txtstream.WriteLine("div")
txtstream.WriteLine("{")
txtstream.WriteLine("    COLOR: white;")
txtstream.WriteLine("    BACKGROUND-COLOR: black;")
txtstream.WriteLine("    FONT-FAMILY: font-family: Cambria, serif;")
txtstream.WriteLine("    FONT-SIZE: 10px;")
txtstream.WriteLine("    text-align: left;")
txtstream.WriteLine("    white-Space: nowrap;")
txtstream.WriteLine("}")
txtstream.WriteLine("span")
txtstream.WriteLine("{")
txtstream.WriteLine("    COLOR: white;")
txtstream.WriteLine("    BACKGROUND-COLOR: black;")
txtstream.WriteLine("    FONT-FAMILY: font-family: Cambria, serif;")
txtstream.WriteLine("    FONT-SIZE: 10px;")
txtstream.WriteLine("    text-align: left;")
```

```
txtstream.WriteLine("    white-Space: nowrap;")
txtstream.WriteLine("    display:inline-block;")
txtstream.WriteLine("    width: 100%;")
txtstream.WriteLine("}")
txtstream.WriteLine("textarea")
txtstream.WriteLine("{")
txtstream.WriteLine("    COLOR: white;")
txtstream.WriteLine("    BACKGROUND-COLOR: black;")
txtstream.WriteLine("    FONT-FAMILY: font-family: Cambria, serif;")
txtstream.WriteLine("    FONT-SIZE: 10px;")
txtstream.WriteLine("    text-align: left;")
txtstream.WriteLine("    white-Space: nowrap;")
txtstream.WriteLine("    width: 100%;")
txtstream.WriteLine("}")
txtstream.WriteLine("select")
txtstream.WriteLine("{")
txtstream.WriteLine("    COLOR: white;")
txtstream.WriteLine("    BACKGROUND-COLOR: black;")
txtstream.WriteLine("    FONT-FAMILY: font-family: Cambria, serif;")
txtstream.WriteLine("    FONT-SIZE: 10px;")
txtstream.WriteLine("    text-align: left;")
txtstream.WriteLine("    white-Space: nowrap;")
txtstream.WriteLine("    width: 100%;")
txtstream.WriteLine("}")
txtstream.WriteLine("input")
txtstream.WriteLine("{")
txtstream.WriteLine("    COLOR: white;")
txtstream.WriteLine("    BACKGROUND-COLOR: black;")
txtstream.WriteLine("    FONT-FAMILY: font-family: Cambria, serif;")
txtstream.WriteLine("    FONT-SIZE: 12px;")
txtstream.WriteLine("    text-align: left;")
txtstream.WriteLine("    display:table-cell;")
txtstream.WriteLine("    white-Space: nowrap;")
```

```
txtstream.WriteLine("}")
txtstream.WriteLine("h1 {")
txtstream.WriteLine("color: antiquewhite;")
txtstream.WriteLine("text-shadow: 1px 1px 1px black;")
txtstream.WriteLine("padding: 3px;")
txtstream.WriteLine("text-align: center;")
txtstream.WriteLine("box-shadow: inset 2px 2px 5px rgba(0,0,0,0.5), inset -2px -2px 5px rgba(255,255,255,0.5);")
txtstream.WriteLine("}")
txtstream.WriteLine("</style>")
```

COLORED TEXT

```
txtstream.WriteLine("<style type='text/css'>")
txtstream.WriteLine("th")
txtstream.WriteLine("{")
txtstream.WriteLine("   COLOR: darkred;")
txtstream.WriteLine("   BACKGROUND-COLOR: #eeeeee;")
txtstream.WriteLine("   FONT-FAMILY:font-family: Cambria, serif;")
txtstream.WriteLine("   FONT-SIZE: 12px;")
txtstream.WriteLine("   text-align: left;")
txtstream.WriteLine("   white-Space: nowrap;")
txtstream.WriteLine("}")
txtstream.WriteLine("td")
txtstream.WriteLine("{")
txtstream.WriteLine("   COLOR: navy;")
txtstream.WriteLine("   BACKGROUND-COLOR: #eeeeee;")
txtstream.WriteLine("   FONT-FAMILY: font-family: Cambria, serif;")
txtstream.WriteLine("   FONT-SIZE: 12px;")
txtstream.WriteLine("   text-align: left;")
txtstream.WriteLine("   white-Space: nowrap;")
txtstream.WriteLine("}")
txtstream.WriteLine("div")
```

```
txtstream.WriteLine("{")
txtstream.WriteLine("   COLOR: white;")
txtstream.WriteLine("   BACKGROUND-COLOR: navy;")
txtstream.WriteLine("   FONT-FAMILY: font-family: Cambria, serif;")
txtstream.WriteLine("   FONT-SIZE: 10px;")
txtstream.WriteLine("   text-align: left;")
txtstream.WriteLine("   white-Space: nowrap;")
txtstream.WriteLine("}")
txtstream.WriteLine("span")
txtstream.WriteLine("{")
txtstream.WriteLine("   COLOR: white;")
txtstream.WriteLine("   BACKGROUND-COLOR: navy;")
txtstream.WriteLine("   FONT-FAMILY: font-family: Cambria, serif;")
txtstream.WriteLine("   FONT-SIZE: 10px;")
txtstream.WriteLine("   text-align: left;")
txtstream.WriteLine("   white-Space: nowrap;")
txtstream.WriteLine("   display:inline-block;")
txtstream.WriteLine("   width: 100%;")
txtstream.WriteLine("}")
txtstream.WriteLine("textarea")
txtstream.WriteLine("{")
txtstream.WriteLine("   COLOR: white;")
txtstream.WriteLine("   BACKGROUND-COLOR: navy;")
txtstream.WriteLine("   FONT-FAMILY: font-family: Cambria, serif;")
txtstream.WriteLine("   FONT-SIZE: 10px;")
txtstream.WriteLine("   text-align: left;")
txtstream.WriteLine("   white-Space: nowrap;")
txtstream.WriteLine("   width: 100%;")
txtstream.WriteLine("}")
txtstream.WriteLine("select")
txtstream.WriteLine("{")
txtstream.WriteLine("   COLOR: white;")
txtstream.WriteLine("   BACKGROUND-COLOR: navy;")
```

```
txtstream.WriteLine("    FONT-FAMILY: font-family: Cambria, serif;")
txtstream.WriteLine("    FONT-SIZE: 10px;")
txtstream.WriteLine("    text-align: left;")
txtstream.WriteLine("    white-Space: nowrap;")
txtstream.WriteLine("    width: 100%;")
txtstream.WriteLine("}")
txtstream.WriteLine("input")
txtstream.WriteLine("{")
txtstream.WriteLine("    COLOR: white;")
txtstream.WriteLine("    BACKGROUND-COLOR: navy;")
txtstream.WriteLine("    FONT-FAMILY: font-family: Cambria, serif;")
txtstream.WriteLine("    FONT-SIZE: 12px;")
txtstream.WriteLine("    text-align: left;")
txtstream.WriteLine("    display:table-cell;")
txtstream.WriteLine("    white-Space: nowrap;")
txtstream.WriteLine("}")
txtstream.WriteLine("h1 {")
txtstream.WriteLine("color: antiquewhite;")
txtstream.WriteLine("text-shadow: 1px 1px 1px black;")
txtstream.WriteLine("padding: 3px;")
txtstream.WriteLine("text-align: center;")
txtstream.WriteLine("box-shadow: inset 2px 2px 5px rgba(0,0,0,0.5), inset -2px -2px 5px rgba(255,255,255,0.5);")
txtstream.WriteLine("}")
txtstream.WriteLine("</style>")
```

OSCILLATING ROW COLORS

```
txtstream.WriteLine("<style>")
txtstream.WriteLine("th")
txtstream.WriteLine("{")
```

```
txtstream.WriteLine("    COLOR: white;")
txtstream.WriteLine("    BACKGROUND-COLOR: navy;")
txtstream.WriteLine("    FONT-FAMILY:font-family: Cambria, serif;")
txtstream.WriteLine("    FONT-SIZE: 12px;")
txtstream.WriteLine("    text-align: left;")
txtstream.WriteLine("    white-Space: nowrap;")
txtstream.WriteLine("}")
txtstream.WriteLine("td")
txtstream.WriteLine("{")
txtstream.WriteLine("    COLOR: navy;")
txtstream.WriteLine("    FONT-FAMILY: font-family: Cambria, serif;")
txtstream.WriteLine("    FONT-SIZE: 12px;")
txtstream.WriteLine("    text-align: left;")
txtstream.WriteLine("    white-Space: nowrap;")
txtstream.WriteLine("}")
txtstream.WriteLine("div")
txtstream.WriteLine("{")
txtstream.WriteLine("    COLOR: navy;")
txtstream.WriteLine("    FONT-FAMILY: font-family: Cambria, serif;")
txtstream.WriteLine("    FONT-SIZE: 12px;")
txtstream.WriteLine("    text-align: left;")
txtstream.WriteLine("    white-Space: nowrap;")
txtstream.WriteLine("}")
txtstream.WriteLine("span")
txtstream.WriteLine("{")
txtstream.WriteLine("    COLOR: navy;")
txtstream.WriteLine("    FONT-FAMILY: font-family: Cambria, serif;")
txtstream.WriteLine("    FONT-SIZE: 12px;")
txtstream.WriteLine("    text-align: left;")
txtstream.WriteLine("    white-Space: nowrap;")
txtstream.WriteLine("    width: 100%;")
txtstream.WriteLine("}")
txtstream.WriteLine("textarea")
```

```
txtstream.WriteLine("{")
txtstream.WriteLine("    COLOR: navy;")
txtstream.WriteLine("    FONT-FAMILY: font-family: Cambria, serif;")
txtstream.WriteLine("    FONT-SIZE: 12px;")
txtstream.WriteLine("    text-align: left;")
txtstream.WriteLine("    white-Space: nowrap;")
txtstream.WriteLine("    display:inline-block;")
txtstream.WriteLine("    width: 100%;")
txtstream.WriteLine("}")
txtstream.WriteLine("select")
txtstream.WriteLine("{")
txtstream.WriteLine("    COLOR: navy;")
txtstream.WriteLine("    FONT-FAMILY: font-family: Cambria, serif;")
txtstream.WriteLine("    FONT-SIZE: 10px;")
txtstream.WriteLine("    text-align: left;")
txtstream.WriteLine("    white-Space: nowrap;")
txtstream.WriteLine("    display:inline-block;")
txtstream.WriteLine("    width: 100%;")
txtstream.WriteLine("}")
txtstream.WriteLine("input")
txtstream.WriteLine("{")
txtstream.WriteLine("    COLOR: navy;")
txtstream.WriteLine("    FONT-FAMILY: font-family: Cambria, serif;")
txtstream.WriteLine("    FONT-SIZE: 12px;")
txtstream.WriteLine("    text-align: left;")
txtstream.WriteLine("    display:table-cell;")
txtstream.WriteLine("    white-Space: nowrap;")
txtstream.WriteLine("}")
txtstream.WriteLine("h1 {")
txtstream.WriteLine("color: antiquewhite;")
txtstream.WriteLine("text-shadow: 1px 1px 1px black;")
txtstream.WriteLine("padding: 3px;")
txtstream.WriteLine("text-align: center;")
```

txtstream.WriteLine("box-shadow: inset 2px 2px 5px rgba(0,0,0,0.5), inset -2px -2px 5px rgba(255,255,255,0.5);")

txtstream.WriteLine("}")

txtstream.WriteLine("tr:nth-child(even){background-color:#f2f2f2;}")

txtstream.WriteLine("tr:nth-child(odd){background-color:#cccccc; color:#f2f2f2;}")

txtstream.WriteLine("</style>")

GHOST DECORATED

txtstream.WriteLine("<style type='text/css'>")

txtstream.WriteLine("th")

txtstream.WriteLine("{")

txtstream.WriteLine("   COLOR: black;")

txtstream.WriteLine("   BACKGROUND-COLOR: white;")

txtstream.WriteLine("   FONT-FAMILY:font-family: Cambria, serif;")

txtstream.WriteLine("   FONT-SIZE: 12px;")

txtstream.WriteLine("   text-align: left;")

txtstream.WriteLine("   white-Space: nowrap;")

txtstream.WriteLine("}")

txtstream.WriteLine("td")

txtstream.WriteLine("{")

txtstream.WriteLine("   COLOR: black;")

txtstream.WriteLine("   BACKGROUND-COLOR: white;")

txtstream.WriteLine("   FONT-FAMILY: font-family: Cambria, serif;")

txtstream.WriteLine("   FONT-SIZE: 12px;")

txtstream.WriteLine("   text-align: left;")

txtstream.WriteLine("   white-Space: nowrap;")

txtstream.WriteLine("}")

txtstream.WriteLine("div")

txtstream.WriteLine("{")

txtstream.WriteLine("   COLOR: black;")

txtstream.WriteLine("   BACKGROUND-COLOR: white;")

```
txtstream.WriteLine("    FONT-FAMILY: font-family: Cambria, serif;")
txtstream.WriteLine("    FONT-SIZE: 10px;")
txtstream.WriteLine("    text-align: left;")
txtstream.WriteLine("    white-Space: nowrap;")
txtstream.WriteLine("}")
txtstream.WriteLine("span")
txtstream.WriteLine("{")
txtstream.WriteLine("    COLOR: black;")
txtstream.WriteLine("    BACKGROUND-COLOR: white;")
txtstream.WriteLine("    FONT-FAMILY: font-family: Cambria, serif;")
txtstream.WriteLine("    FONT-SIZE: 10px;")
txtstream.WriteLine("    text-align: left;")
txtstream.WriteLine("    white-Space: nowrap;")
txtstream.WriteLine("    display:inline-block;")
txtstream.WriteLine("    width: 100%;")
txtstream.WriteLine("}")
txtstream.WriteLine("textarea")
txtstream.WriteLine("{")
txtstream.WriteLine("    COLOR: black;")
txtstream.WriteLine("    BACKGROUND-COLOR: white;")
txtstream.WriteLine("    FONT-FAMILY: font-family: Cambria, serif;")
txtstream.WriteLine("    FONT-SIZE: 10px;")
txtstream.WriteLine("    text-align: left;")
txtstream.WriteLine("    white-Space: nowrap;")
txtstream.WriteLine("    width: 100%;")
txtstream.WriteLine("}")
txtstream.WriteLine("select")
txtstream.WriteLine("{")
txtstream.WriteLine("    COLOR: black;")
txtstream.WriteLine("    BACKGROUND-COLOR: white;")
txtstream.WriteLine("    FONT-FAMILY: font-family: Cambria, serif;")
txtstream.WriteLine("    FONT-SIZE: 10px;")
txtstream.WriteLine("    text-align: left;")
```

```
txtstream.WriteLine("    white-Space: nowrap;")
txtstream.WriteLine("    width: 100%;")
txtstream.WriteLine("}")
txtstream.WriteLine("input")
txtstream.WriteLine("{")
txtstream.WriteLine("    COLOR: black;")
txtstream.WriteLine("    BACKGROUND-COLOR: white;")
txtstream.WriteLine("    FONT-FAMILY: font-family: Cambria, serif;")
txtstream.WriteLine("    FONT-SIZE: 12px;")
txtstream.WriteLine("    text-align: left;")
txtstream.WriteLine("    display:table-cell;")
txtstream.WriteLine("    white-Space: nowrap;")
txtstream.WriteLine("}")
txtstream.WriteLine("h1 {")
txtstream.WriteLine("color: antiquewhite;")
txtstream.WriteLine("text-shadow: 1px 1px 1px black;")
txtstream.WriteLine("padding: 3px;")
txtstream.WriteLine("text-align: center;")
txtstream.WriteLine("box-shadow: inset 2px 2px 5px rgba(0,0,0,0.5), inset -
2px -2px 5px rgba(255,255,255,0.5);")
txtstream.WriteLine("}")
txtstream.WriteLine("</style>")
```

3D

```
txtstream.WriteLine("<style type='text/css'>")
txtstream.WriteLine("body")
txtstream.WriteLine("{")
txtstream.WriteLine("    PADDING-RIGHT: 0px;")
txtstream.WriteLine("    PADDING-LEFT: 0px;")
txtstream.WriteLine("    PADDING-BOTTOM: 0px;")
txtstream.WriteLine("    MARGIN: 0px;")
```

```
txtstream.WriteLine("    COLOR: #333;")
txtstream.WriteLine("    PADDING-TOP: 0px;")
txtstream.WriteLine("    FONT-FAMILY: verdana, arial, helvetica, sans-serif;")
txtstream.WriteLine("}")
txtstream.WriteLine("table")
txtstream.WriteLine("{")
txtstream.WriteLine("    BORDER-RIGHT: #999999 3px solid;")
txtstream.WriteLine("    PADDING-RIGHT: 6px;")
txtstream.WriteLine("    PADDING-LEFT: 6px;")
txtstream.WriteLine("    FONT-WEIGHT: Bold;")
txtstream.WriteLine("    FONT-SIZE: 14px;")
txtstream.WriteLine("    PADDING-BOTTOM: 6px;")
txtstream.WriteLine("    COLOR: Peru;")
txtstream.WriteLine("    LINE-HEIGHT: 14px;")
txtstream.WriteLine("    PADDING-TOP: 6px;")
txtstream.WriteLine("    BORDER-BOTTOM: #999 1px solid;")
txtstream.WriteLine("    BACKGROUND-COLOR: #eeeeee;")
txtstream.WriteLine("    FONT-FAMILY: verdana, arial, helvetica, sans-serif;")
txtstream.WriteLine("    FONT-SIZE: 12px;")
txtstream.WriteLine("}")
txtstream.WriteLine("th")
txtstream.WriteLine("{")
txtstream.WriteLine("    BORDER-RIGHT: #999999 3px solid;")
txtstream.WriteLine("    PADDING-RIGHT: 6px;")
txtstream.WriteLine("    PADDING-LEFT: 6px;")
txtstream.WriteLine("    FONT-WEIGHT: Bold;")
txtstream.WriteLine("    FONT-SIZE: 14px;")
txtstream.WriteLine("    PADDING-BOTTOM: 6px;")
txtstream.WriteLine("    COLOR: darkred;")
txtstream.WriteLine("    LINE-HEIGHT: 14px;")
txtstream.WriteLine("    PADDING-TOP: 6px;")
txtstream.WriteLine("    BORDER-BOTTOM: #999 1px solid;")
txtstream.WriteLine("    BACKGROUND-COLOR: #eeeeee;")
```

```
txtstream.WriteLine("    FONT-FAMILY:font-family: Cambria, serif;")
txtstream.WriteLine("    FONT-SIZE: 12px;")
txtstream.WriteLine("    text-align: left;")
txtstream.WriteLine("    white-Space: nowrap;")
txtstream.WriteLine("}")
txtstream.WriteLine(".th")
txtstream.WriteLine("{")
txtstream.WriteLine("    BORDER-RIGHT: #999999 2px solid;")
txtstream.WriteLine("    PADDING-RIGHT: 6px;")
txtstream.WriteLine("    PADDING-LEFT: 6px;")
txtstream.WriteLine("    FONT-WEIGHT: Bold;")
txtstream.WriteLine("    PADDING-BOTTOM: 6px;")
txtstream.WriteLine("    COLOR: black;")
txtstream.WriteLine("    PADDING-TOP: 6px;")
txtstream.WriteLine("    BORDER-BOTTOM: #999 2px solid;")
txtstream.WriteLine("    BACKGROUND-COLOR: #eeeeee;")
txtstream.WriteLine("    FONT-FAMILY: font-family: Cambria, serif;")
txtstream.WriteLine("    FONT-SIZE: 10px;")
txtstream.WriteLine("    text-align: right;")
txtstream.WriteLine("    white-Space: nowrap;")
txtstream.WriteLine("}")
txtstream.WriteLine("td")
txtstream.WriteLine("{")
txtstream.WriteLine("    BORDER-RIGHT: #999999 3px solid;")
txtstream.WriteLine("    PADDING-RIGHT: 6px;")
txtstream.WriteLine("    PADDING-LEFT: 6px;")
txtstream.WriteLine("    FONT-WEIGHT: Normal;")
txtstream.WriteLine("    PADDING-BOTTOM: 6px;")
txtstream.WriteLine("    COLOR: navy;")
txtstream.WriteLine("    LINE-HEIGHT: 14px;")
txtstream.WriteLine("    PADDING-TOP: 6px;")
txtstream.WriteLine("    BORDER-BOTTOM: #999 1px solid;")
txtstream.WriteLine("    BACKGROUND-COLOR: #eeeeee;")
```

```
txtstream.WriteLine("    FONT-FAMILY: font-family: Cambria, serif;")
txtstream.WriteLine("    FONT-SIZE: 12px;")
txtstream.WriteLine("    text-align: left;")
txtstream.WriteLine("    white-Space: nowrap;")
txtstream.WriteLine("}")
txtstream.WriteLine("div")
txtstream.WriteLine("{")
txtstream.WriteLine("    BORDER-RIGHT: #999999 3px solid;")
txtstream.WriteLine("    PADDING-RIGHT: 6px;")
txtstream.WriteLine("    PADDING-LEFT: 6px;")
txtstream.WriteLine("    FONT-WEIGHT: Normal;")
txtstream.WriteLine("    PADDING-BOTTOM: 6px;")
txtstream.WriteLine("    COLOR: white;")
txtstream.WriteLine("    PADDING-TOP: 6px;")
txtstream.WriteLine("    BORDER-BOTTOM: #999 1px solid;")
txtstream.WriteLine("    BACKGROUND-COLOR: navy;")
txtstream.WriteLine("    FONT-FAMILY: font-family: Cambria, serif;")
txtstream.WriteLine("    FONT-SIZE: 10px;")
txtstream.WriteLine("    text-align: left;")
txtstream.WriteLine("    white-Space: nowrap;")
txtstream.WriteLine("}")
txtstream.WriteLine("span")
txtstream.WriteLine("{")
txtstream.WriteLine("    BORDER-RIGHT: #999999 3px solid;")
txtstream.WriteLine("    PADDING-RIGHT: 3px;")
txtstream.WriteLine("    PADDING-LEFT: 3px;")
txtstream.WriteLine("    FONT-WEIGHT: Normal;")
txtstream.WriteLine("    PADDING-BOTTOM: 3px;")
txtstream.WriteLine("    COLOR: white;")
txtstream.WriteLine("    PADDING-TOP: 3px;")
txtstream.WriteLine("    BORDER-BOTTOM: #999 1px solid;")
txtstream.WriteLine("    BACKGROUND-COLOR: navy;")
txtstream.WriteLine("    FONT-FAMILY: font-family: Cambria, serif;")
```

```
txtstream.WriteLine("    FONT-SIZE: 10px;")
txtstream.WriteLine("    text-align: left;")
txtstream.WriteLine("    white-Space: nowrap;")
txtstream.WriteLine("    display:inline-block;")
txtstream.WriteLine("    width: 100%;")
txtstream.WriteLine("}")
txtstream.WriteLine("textarea")
txtstream.WriteLine("{")
txtstream.WriteLine("    BORDER-RIGHT: #999999 3px solid;")
txtstream.WriteLine("    PADDING-RIGHT: 3px;")
txtstream.WriteLine("    PADDING-LEFT: 3px;")
txtstream.WriteLine("    FONT-WEIGHT: Normal;")
txtstream.WriteLine("    PADDING-BOTTOM: 3px;")
txtstream.WriteLine("    COLOR: white;")
txtstream.WriteLine("    PADDING-TOP: 3px;")
txtstream.WriteLine("    BORDER-BOTTOM: #999 1px solid;")
txtstream.WriteLine("    BACKGROUND-COLOR: navy;")
txtstream.WriteLine("    FONT-FAMILY: font-family: Cambria, serif;")
txtstream.WriteLine("    FONT-SIZE: 10px;")
txtstream.WriteLine("    text-align: left;")
txtstream.WriteLine("    white-Space: nowrap;")
txtstream.WriteLine("    width: 100%;")
txtstream.WriteLine("}")
txtstream.WriteLine("select")
txtstream.WriteLine("{")
txtstream.WriteLine("    BORDER-RIGHT: #999999 3px solid;")
txtstream.WriteLine("    PADDING-RIGHT: 6px;")
txtstream.WriteLine("    PADDING-LEFT: 6px;")
txtstream.WriteLine("    FONT-WEIGHT: Normal;")
txtstream.WriteLine("    PADDING-BOTTOM: 6px;")
txtstream.WriteLine("    COLOR: white;")
txtstream.WriteLine("    PADDING-TOP: 6px;")
txtstream.WriteLine("    BORDER-BOTTOM: #999 1px solid;")
```

```
txtstream.WriteLine("    BACKGROUND-COLOR: navy;")
txtstream.WriteLine("    FONT-FAMILY: font-family: Cambria, serif;")
txtstream.WriteLine("    FONT-SIZE: 10px;")
txtstream.WriteLine("    text-align: left;")
txtstream.WriteLine("    white-Space: nowrap;")
txtstream.WriteLine("    width: 100%;")
txtstream.WriteLine("}")
txtstream.WriteLine("input")
txtstream.WriteLine("{")
txtstream.WriteLine("    BORDER-RIGHT: #999999 3px solid;")
txtstream.WriteLine("    PADDING-RIGHT: 3px;")
txtstream.WriteLine("    PADDING-LEFT: 3px;")
txtstream.WriteLine("    FONT-WEIGHT: Bold;")
txtstream.WriteLine("    PADDING-BOTTOM: 3px;")
txtstream.WriteLine("    COLOR: white;")
txtstream.WriteLine("    PADDING-TOP: 3px;")
txtstream.WriteLine("    BORDER-BOTTOM: #999 1px solid;")
txtstream.WriteLine("    BACKGROUND-COLOR: navy;")
txtstream.WriteLine("    FONT-FAMILY: font-family: Cambria, serif;")
txtstream.WriteLine("    FONT-SIZE: 12px;")
txtstream.WriteLine("    text-align: left;")
txtstream.WriteLine("    display:table-cell;")
txtstream.WriteLine("    white-Space: nowrap;")
txtstream.WriteLine("    width: 100%;")
txtstream.WriteLine("}")
txtstream.WriteLine("h1 {")
txtstream.WriteLine("color: antiquewhite;")
txtstream.WriteLine("text-shadow: 1px 1px 1px black;")
txtstream.WriteLine("padding: 3px;")
txtstream.WriteLine("text-align: center;")
txtstream.WriteLine("box-shadow: inset 2px 2px 5px rgba(0,0,0,0.5), inset -2px -2px 5px rgba(255,255,255,0.5);")
txtstream.WriteLine("}")
```

```
txtstream.WriteLine("</style>")
```

SHADOW BOX

```
txtstream.WriteLine("<style type='text/css'>")
txtstream.WriteLine("body")
txtstream.WriteLine("{")
txtstream.WriteLine("    PADDING-RIGHT: 0px;")
txtstream.WriteLine("    PADDING-LEFT: 0px;")
txtstream.WriteLine("    PADDING-BOTTOM: 0px;")
txtstream.WriteLine("    MARGIN: 0px;")
txtstream.WriteLine("    COLOR: #333;")
txtstream.WriteLine("    PADDING-TOP: 0px;")
txtstream.WriteLine("    FONT-FAMILY: verdana, arial, helvetica, sans-serif;")
txtstream.WriteLine("}")
txtstream.WriteLine("table")
txtstream.WriteLine("{")
txtstream.WriteLine("    BORDER-RIGHT: #999999 1px solid;")
txtstream.WriteLine("    PADDING-RIGHT: 1px;")
txtstream.WriteLine("    PADDING-LEFT: 1px;")
txtstream.WriteLine("    PADDING-BOTTOM: 1px;")
txtstream.WriteLine("    LINE-HEIGHT: 8px;")
txtstream.WriteLine("    PADDING-TOP: 1px;")
txtstream.WriteLine("    BORDER-BOTTOM: #999 1px solid;")
txtstream.WriteLine("    BACKGROUND-COLOR: #eeeeee;")
txtstream.WriteLine("
filter:progid:DXImageTransform.Microsoft.Shadow(color='silver',    Direction=135,
Strength=16")
txtstream.WriteLine("}")
txtstream.WriteLine("th")
txtstream.WriteLine("{")
txtstream.WriteLine("    BORDER-RIGHT: #999999 3px solid;")
txtstream.WriteLine("    PADDING-RIGHT: 6px;")
```

```
txtstream.WriteLine("    PADDING-LEFT: 6px;")
txtstream.WriteLine("    FONT-WEIGHT: Bold;")
txtstream.WriteLine("    FONT-SIZE: 14px;")
txtstream.WriteLine("    PADDING-BOTTOM: 6px;")
txtstream.WriteLine("    COLOR: darkred;")
txtstream.WriteLine("    LINE-HEIGHT: 14px;")
txtstream.WriteLine("    PADDING-TOP: 6px;")
txtstream.WriteLine("    BORDER-BOTTOM: #999 1px solid;")
txtstream.WriteLine("    BACKGROUND-COLOR: #eeeeee;")
txtstream.WriteLine("    FONT-FAMILY: font-family: Cambria, serif;")
txtstream.WriteLine("    FONT-SIZE: 12px;")
txtstream.WriteLine("    text-align: left;")
txtstream.WriteLine("    white-Space: nowrap;")
txtstream.WriteLine("}")
txtstream.WriteLine(".th")
txtstream.WriteLine("{")
txtstream.WriteLine("    BORDER-RIGHT: #999999 2px solid;")
txtstream.WriteLine("    PADDING-RIGHT: 6px;")
txtstream.WriteLine("    PADDING-LEFT: 6px;")
txtstream.WriteLine("    FONT-WEIGHT: Bold;")
txtstream.WriteLine("    PADDING-BOTTOM: 6px;")
txtstream.WriteLine("    COLOR: black;")
txtstream.WriteLine("    PADDING-TOP: 6px;")
txtstream.WriteLine("    BORDER-BOTTOM: #999 2px solid;")
txtstream.WriteLine("    BACKGROUND-COLOR: #eeeeee;")
txtstream.WriteLine("    FONT-FAMILY: font-family: Cambria, serif;")
txtstream.WriteLine("    FONT-SIZE: 10px;")
txtstream.WriteLine("    text-align: right;")
txtstream.WriteLine("    white-Space: nowrap;")
txtstream.WriteLine("}")
txtstream.WriteLine("td")
txtstream.WriteLine("{")
txtstream.WriteLine("    BORDER-RIGHT: #999999 3px solid;")
```

```
txtstream.WriteLine("    PADDING-RIGHT: 6px;")
txtstream.WriteLine("    PADDING-LEFT: 6px;")
txtstream.WriteLine("    FONT-WEIGHT: Normal;")
txtstream.WriteLine("    PADDING-BOTTOM: 6px;")
txtstream.WriteLine("    COLOR: navy;")
txtstream.WriteLine("    LINE-HEIGHT: 14px;")
txtstream.WriteLine("    PADDING-TOP: 6px;")
txtstream.WriteLine("    BORDER-BOTTOM: #999 1px solid;")
txtstream.WriteLine("    BACKGROUND-COLOR: #eeeeee;")
txtstream.WriteLine("    FONT-FAMILY: font-family: Cambria, serif;")
txtstream.WriteLine("    FONT-SIZE: 12px;")
txtstream.WriteLine("    text-align: left;")
txtstream.WriteLine("    white-Space: nowrap;")
txtstream.WriteLine("}")
txtstream.WriteLine("div")
txtstream.WriteLine("{")
txtstream.WriteLine("    BORDER-RIGHT: #999999 3px solid;")
txtstream.WriteLine("    PADDING-RIGHT: 6px;")
txtstream.WriteLine("    PADDING-LEFT: 6px;")
txtstream.WriteLine("    FONT-WEIGHT: Normal;")
txtstream.WriteLine("    PADDING-BOTTOM: 6px;")
txtstream.WriteLine("    COLOR: white;")
txtstream.WriteLine("    PADDING-TOP: 6px;")
txtstream.WriteLine("    BORDER-BOTTOM: #999 1px solid;")
txtstream.WriteLine("    BACKGROUND-COLOR: navy;")
txtstream.WriteLine("    FONT-FAMILY: font-family: Cambria, serif;")
txtstream.WriteLine("    FONT-SIZE: 10px;")
txtstream.WriteLine("    text-align: left;")
txtstream.WriteLine("    white-Space: nowrap;")
txtstream.WriteLine("}")
txtstream.WriteLine("span")
txtstream.WriteLine("{")
txtstream.WriteLine("    BORDER-RIGHT: #999999 3px solid;")
```

```
txtstream.WriteLine("    PADDING-RIGHT: 3px;")
txtstream.WriteLine("    PADDING-LEFT: 3px;")
txtstream.WriteLine("    FONT-WEIGHT: Normal;")
txtstream.WriteLine("    PADDING-BOTTOM: 3px;")
txtstream.WriteLine("    COLOR: white;")
txtstream.WriteLine("    PADDING-TOP: 3px;")
txtstream.WriteLine("    BORDER-BOTTOM: #999 1px solid;")
txtstream.WriteLine("    BACKGROUND-COLOR: navy;")
txtstream.WriteLine("    FONT-FAMILY: font-family: Cambria, serif;")
txtstream.WriteLine("    FONT-SIZE: 10px;")
txtstream.WriteLine("    text-align: left;")
txtstream.WriteLine("    white-Space: nowrap;")
txtstream.WriteLine("    display: inline-block;")
txtstream.WriteLine("    width: 100%;")
txtstream.WriteLine("}")
txtstream.WriteLine("textarea")
txtstream.WriteLine("{")
txtstream.WriteLine("    BORDER-RIGHT: #999999 3px solid;")
txtstream.WriteLine("    PADDING-RIGHT: 3px;")
txtstream.WriteLine("    PADDING-LEFT: 3px;")
txtstream.WriteLine("    FONT-WEIGHT: Normal;")
txtstream.WriteLine("    PADDING-BOTTOM: 3px;")
txtstream.WriteLine("    COLOR: white;")
txtstream.WriteLine("    PADDING-TOP: 3px;")
txtstream.WriteLine("    BORDER-BOTTOM: #999 1px solid;")
txtstream.WriteLine("    BACKGROUND-COLOR: navy;")
txtstream.WriteLine("    FONT-FAMILY: font-family: Cambria, serif;")
txtstream.WriteLine("    FONT-SIZE: 10px;")
txtstream.WriteLine("    text-align: left;")
txtstream.WriteLine("    white-Space: nowrap;")
txtstream.WriteLine("    width: 100%;")
txtstream.WriteLine("}")
txtstream.WriteLine("select")
```

```
txtstream.WriteLine("{")
txtstream.WriteLine("   BORDER-RIGHT: #999999 3px solid;")
txtstream.WriteLine("   PADDING-RIGHT: 6px;")
txtstream.WriteLine("   PADDING-LEFT: 6px;")
txtstream.WriteLine("   FONT-WEIGHT: Normal;")
txtstream.WriteLine("   PADDING-BOTTOM: 6px;")
txtstream.WriteLine("   COLOR: white;")
txtstream.WriteLine("   PADDING-TOP: 6px;")
txtstream.WriteLine("   BORDER-BOTTOM: #999 1px solid;")
txtstream.WriteLine("   BACKGROUND-COLOR: navy;")
txtstream.WriteLine("   FONT-FAMILY: font-family: Cambria, serif;")
txtstream.WriteLine("   FONT-SIZE: 10px;")
txtstream.WriteLine("   text-align: left;")
txtstream.WriteLine("   white-Space: nowrap;")
txtstream.WriteLine("   width: 100%;")
txtstream.WriteLine("}")
txtstream.WriteLine("input")
txtstream.WriteLine("{")
txtstream.WriteLine("   BORDER-RIGHT: #999999 3px solid;")
txtstream.WriteLine("   PADDING-RIGHT: 3px;")
txtstream.WriteLine("   PADDING-LEFT: 3px;")
txtstream.WriteLine("   FONT-WEIGHT: Bold;")
txtstream.WriteLine("   PADDING-BOTTOM: 3px;")
txtstream.WriteLine("   COLOR: white;")
txtstream.WriteLine("   PADDING-TOP: 3px;")
txtstream.WriteLine("   BORDER-BOTTOM: #999 1px solid;")
txtstream.WriteLine("   BACKGROUND-COLOR: navy;")
txtstream.WriteLine("   FONT-FAMILY: font-family: Cambria, serif;")
txtstream.WriteLine("   FONT-SIZE: 12px;")
txtstream.WriteLine("   text-align: left;")
txtstream.WriteLine("   display: table-cell;")
txtstream.WriteLine("   white-Space: nowrap;")
txtstream.WriteLine("   width: 100%;")
```

```
txtstream.WriteLine("}")
txtstream.WriteLine("h1 {")
txtstream.WriteLine("color: antiquewhite;")
txtstream.WriteLine("text-shadow: 1px 1px 1px black;")
txtstream.WriteLine("padding: 3px;")
txtstream.WriteLine("text-align: center;")
txtstream.WriteLine("box-shadow: inset 2px 2px 5px rgba(0,0,0,0.5), inset -2px -2px 5px rgba(255,255,255,0.5);")
txtstream.WriteLine("}")
txtstream.WriteLine("</style>")
```

www.ingramcontent.com/pod-product-compliance
Lightning Source LLC
Chambersburg PA
CBHW071550080326
40690CB00056B/1626